VOCABULARY
NINJA

ANDREW JENNINGS

BLOOMSBURY EDUCATION

LONDON OXFORD NEW YORK NEW DELHI SYDNEY

BLOOMSBURY EDUCATION
Bloomsbury Publishing Plc
50 Bedford Square, London, WC1B 3DP, UK

BLOOMSBURY, BLOOMSBURY EDUCATION and the Diana logo are trademarks of
Bloomsbury Publishing Plc

First published in Great Britain, 2019 by Bloomsbury Publishing Plc
Text copyright © Andrew Jennings, 2019

A catalogue record for this book is available from the British Library

ISBN: PB: 978-1-4729-6443-4

6 8 10 9 7

Text design by Marcus Duck

Printed and bound in the UK by Ashford Colour Press

All papers used by Bloomsbury Publishing Plc are natural, recyclable products from wood
grown in well managed forests. The manufacturing processes conform to the environmental
regulations of the country of origin

To find out more about our authors and books visit www.bloomsbury.com and sign up for
our newsletters

Acknowledgments

With thanks to Doug Harper for his kind permission to adapt extracts from
The Online Etymology Dictionary (www.etymonline.com) for the
Enthralling etymology section, p97.

To my amazing wife, Claire, our special twins who changed everything for the better, and Max, Marmalade and Peaches. If only words could help me describe my love for you all.

CONTENTS

PART 1 – THE WAY OF THE VOCABULARY NINJA

1 – Welcome, Grasshopper!	9
2 – Problems, solutions and being a Vocabulary Ninja	13
3 – Taught vs encountered vocabulary	22
4 – Explicit vocabulary instruction	33
5 – The vocabulary environment – your classroom	37

PART 2 – VOCABULARY NINJA TEACHING TOOLKIT

Word of the day	44
Vocabulary laboratory	49
Conjunction malfunction	53
Which sentence?	56
Noun vs verb	59
SPaG facts and SPaG spotter	61
CUTS – circle, underline, tick, state	65
Picture processor	68
Vocabulary vault	71
Enthralling etymology	97
Scintillating synonyms	106
Adventurous alternatives	114

PART 3 – BE THE VOCABULARY NINJA

Conclusion	122
Additional resources	123
Answers	124

ONLINE RESOURCES

All resources referenced within this book have been created to be photocopied. Each resource is also available on the Vocabulary Ninja website.

Go to www.vocabularyninja.co.uk and find the book section. Enter the following case sensitive passcode to gain access: Bloomsbury2019

You can find even more information about
Vocabulary Ninja here:
Website – www.vocabularyninja.com
Blog – vocabularyninja.wordpress.com
Twitter – @VocabularyNinja
Twitter – @MrJenningsA

VOCAB LAB APP

The app offers an exciting and engaging way for pupils to explore vocabulary and the possible alternatives for common vocabulary choices. The app contains over 600 alternatives, supported by a child-friendly layout. Simply visit the App Store on your iPad™ and download the app for free. Search for "Vocab Lab".

VOCABULARY NINJA WORD OF THE DAY APP

A new Word of the day is released every day! You can get the Word of the day straight to your smartphone or tablet, making Word of the day even more accessible on the go or in school. It's perfect for supporting your immersive classroom environment, where every word counts.

SENTENCE SAMURAI

A unique whole-school modeling tool for writing and sentence construction. The app models the expansion of basic sentences to more complex and detailed ones. Each set of sentences has been carefully written to match the National Curriculum's writing requirements and expectations of each year group – Year 1 through to Year 6 in one app!

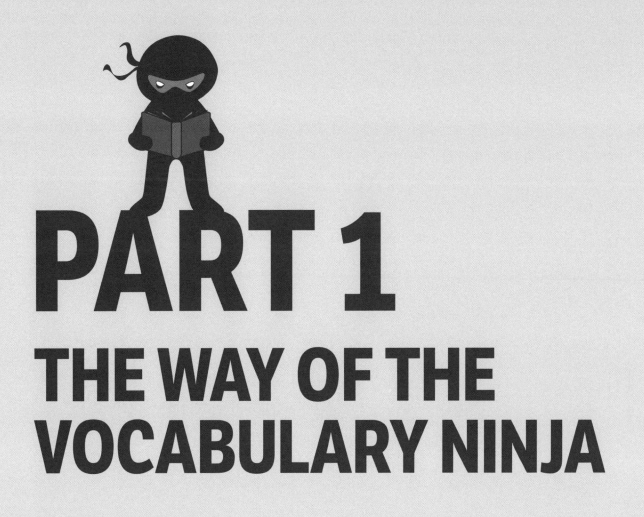

PART 1
THE WAY OF THE VOCABULARY NINJA

1 – WELCOME, GRASSHOPPER

Willkommen, Salve, Bienvenue, Degemer Mat, Mu Amuhezen, Aloha, Maeva, Wellkumma, Salamat Datang, Bon Bini, Benvnuwe, Maayong Pag-Abot, Wolkom, Mauya, Ennidos, **Welcome, Grasshopper.**

WHY SHOULD YOU READ THIS BOOK?

Words and vocabulary are much more than just a piece of the educational jigsaw; words are a constant. Since the beginning of mankind, language and words have evolved with us and are the lifeblood of humanity. Vocabulary surrounds, engulfs and guides us every day; without words, we'd be lost. They are the subconscious map that guides us though day-to-day life, helping us navigate the physical world we live in. It's something we don't think about – it's natural. Even now, reading this book, you're taking it for granted. Actually, words are a privilege. Without words, we would be without enchanting literature, vital historical records, uniquely vibrant and diverse languages, loving conversations, mythical stories and inspirational song lyrics. Words are truly magical, they connect us at a deeper level. What would life be without words?

The purpose of this book is to open your eyes to the power that words have, both inside and outside of the classroom. A learner's understanding, knowledge and control of vocabulary has the power to unlock these learning doors and open them wide. Sadly, for many pupils, these learning doors can remain locked shut, rusted at the hinges, and vocabulary begins to become a significant barrier not just to learning, but to social interactions, communication, self-esteem, mental health and much more. Let's not allow vocabulary to be a subconscious element of your classroom that passes everyone by. Vocabulary must be at the conscious forefront, the frontline force of every conversation, every lesson, every interaction in your school and classroom.

Grasshopper! Welcome and congratulations on beginning your epic journey towards becoming a Vocabulary Ninja Grand Master. At the simplest level, being a Vocabulary Ninja is about making words a priority in your classroom, empowering your pupils, having fun and enriching your whole school. Right from the outset though, it's important to understand that it starts with you. You have to be the leader, the modeller, the fun-maker, the person who makes mistakes and revels in it, the exemplar and the advocate. You have to be the Vocabulary Ninja for your pupils, and they will become your Grasshoppers. By 'mastering vocabulary' with *Vocabulary Ninja*, you will be igniting every area of your curriculum and be developing more independent and confident learners, as well as developing yourself.

As with anything that is worthwhile doing or that is to have any significant impact, it will take time. A marginal gains mentality is required. By keenly focusing on all of the smaller parts – 0.5 per cent here and 0.7 per cent there – we can slowly start to improve progress, standards and outcomes for all learners. To truly master vocabulary, we need to look at every aspect of learning and understand that all of the small parts will eventually add up to something really special. While walking along the corridor, how you speak to pupils and adults, at lunchtimes, greeting pupils, assemblies and in lessons – every aspect is hugely important. You have to become a Vocabulary Ninja. One who is ready to pounce on every opportunity throughout the whole school day, not just in an English lesson starter. (That wouldn't be ninja!) We will talk about marginal gains and micro-ambitions in greater detail in later chapters, and about how we can begin to be micro-successful.

This resource will provide you with a plethora of evidence, practical strategies, engaging games, resources and advice on how to bring words to life in your classroom and open up the doors to a world of understanding. It's one decision you will never regret!

TAKING RESPONSIBILITY FOR VOCABULARY LEARNING

Imagine this scenario: a pupil comes into your lesson wanting to learn but doesn't understand a word or two. Not a huge problem, right? Well, just think of yourself in a meeting or professional development session. The person speaking is using a range of vocabulary that you are unfamiliar with. We've all been there – it's frustrating and you can feel like the session is passing you by so you just switch off altogether. And you're an educated adult. Now go back to the pupil. This pupil might encounter this same scenario every single lesson, every day – switched off in a significant number of lessons because of previous experiences and the fact that vocabulary is a constant barrier. Still not a huge problem? Wrong. Most certainly you will be able to think of a pupil you are teaching or have taught for whom this is true. This is a real problem, and it's getting worse. As educators, we need to investigate the root causes of barriers to learning and try to unpick them; vocabulary, and a lack of it, has the power to slam the learning doors closed – permanently.

All of the blame for poor vocabulary can't be put solely at the doorstep of the learner (a child). Yes, here it comes: we are just as culpable. How often have you started to teach a lesson, used a worksheet, read a text or put a test in front of a pupil and the barrier to them being successful in the given task isn't their mathematical or scientific knowledge, it's the vocabulary, whether it be in the questions or the task itself? What makes this even worse in a lot of cases is that this cycle just repeats and repeats. Think about how demoralising this must be and imagine how you would feel. You can easily empathise and realise how quickly a learner could be switched off and demoralised. This child's progress in learning and negative behaviour traits can become serious issues. Think about pupils where vocabulary has been neglected for years – for their whole life. We can all think of these pupils. Think of all of the time that is invested in managing or trying to transform their behaviour, ultimately with no real impact. Maybe we need to rethink where we invest our attentions and rethink what we value and prioritise. In fact, there's no 'maybe' about it – we *must* rethink how we approach vocabulary.

READING FOR WRITING

If we think about some of our more successful learners, a broad generalisation would suggest they are competent readers. We always talk about how our successful writers are readers. 'You can tell they are a reader,' teachers say. But, if we think about this in more detail, how does reading transcend all other areas of learning? Well, quite simply, our more successful writers read more often, read more advanced texts than their peers, have conversations about reading and the words they encounter, and so have a vast repertoire of vocabulary that they understand and can actively draw upon. An analogy might look a little like this: there are two horses in a race over a mile. Let's call the race, the 'Vocabulary Stakes'. One horse has 40 fences to hurdle along the way, the other has none.

In reality, the race is a lesson, learning and understanding are what's at stake and the handicap is vocabulary. Who's going to win? With the 'stakes' so high, can we afford for the race to be a handicap? The analogy is a sad one because it depicts learners as lone runners. We need to ensure that we act so that our learning race is run together, 'obstacle course' style. We know it's going to get dirty, there'll be a few scraped knees along the way, but regardless of how strong each individual is, some of the obstacles will be insurmountable alone. We will only be successful together.

As educators, we need to evaluate how we prepare and facilitate our learners for this learning race and plan to minimise the hurdles that they have to encounter. The first step is acknowledging that vocabulary does create a huge barrier and that we need to do something about it. Having an obstacle course mentality is another great analogy to apply to our mindset as educators, as we start to think about how we will go about making vocabulary a core focus within our classrooms. The barriers that we will face as educators will be constant and varied; there is no short-cut, no quick fix and no hack. Once we accept this, we can be better prepared to rise to the challenge on a day-to-day, lesson-by-lesson and minute-by-minute basis.

VOCABULARY NINJA ROLE ON THE WALL
THE NINJA MENTALITY

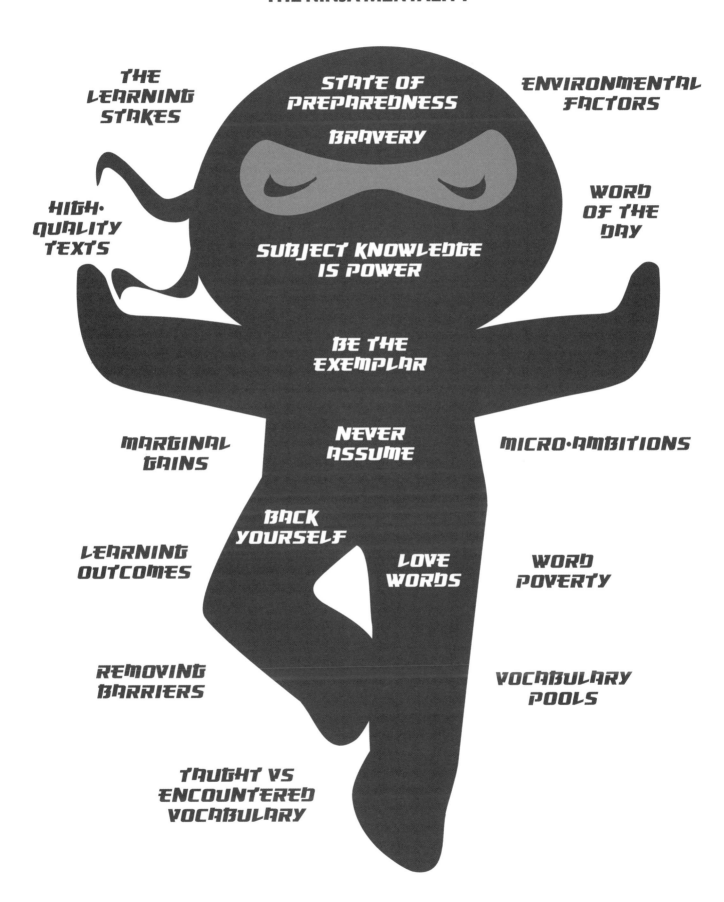

ASPIRE TO INSPIRE

This book will equip you with the basics by providing you with a huge arsenal of practical ideas, lessons, games, resources, strategies and content to start your vocabulary journey in school, and, if I dare say it, without getting bogged down in too much theory (just a sprinkling will do). It would be quite easy to talk about vocabulary being a huge barrier to understanding for pupils and then not apply it to this book for you as a reader. This book isn't going to baffle you with big words and challenging theories, as vocabulary might do for pupils in the classroom. I won't apologise for this simplistic approach – I don't intend on becoming a hypocrite. *Vocabulary Ninja* simply aspires to inspire other teaching practitioners to make vocabulary a priority that underpins all other teaching. As a full-time teacher myself, I know first-hand the significant impact that immersing learners in a vocabulary-oriented environment can have!

VOCABULARY NINJA ROLE ON THE WALL

The Vocabulary Ninja Role on the wall poster (page 11) is your visual guide to the content found throughout this book. More importantly, the Vocabulary Ninja Role on the wall poster is a reference point for your own journey to becoming more Vocabulary Ninja and the type of mentality that you must adopt. It is also a reminder that, even on the toughest of days, you are awesome and you got this! By being more aware of your own state of mind and the external influences that can impact upon it, you can be better prepared to be even more awesome every day, and not sweat the small stuff. Even by coming this far, I know you are ready to make every day better for yourself and your pupils!

As with a traditional role on the wall activity, the words outside the ninja allude to the external, social, cultural and environmental factors that you will need to consider and understand as you progress through your journey of enlightenment.

The interior of the ninja is less cluttered, more orderly and focused. This is exactly how we need to be, as teachers. On the outside we have external factors that will constantly fluctuate in frequency and intensity, whereas we have a greater degree of control of our thoughts and attitudes towards the day, teaching and vocabulary.

All of the factors identified on the Vocabulary Ninja Role on the wall poster impact on your overall effectiveness and your overall awesomeness. A better understanding of each factor and its potential impact will allow you to be more ninja each and every day!

2 – PROBLEMS, SOLUTIONS AND BEING A VOCABULARY NINJA

This chapter explores some of the reasons why pupils' vocabularies might be limited and what the impact of this could be. The chapter also promotes the importance of developing your own 'Vocabulary Ninja' teaching mentality as the first step towards effectively bringing vocabulary to life in your classroom.

These are the mere ramblings of a Vocabulary Ninja, my pearls of wisdom, advice and spiritual guidance. Beyond all of this, the chapter aims to provoke you. Provoke you into thinking about yourself, your ambitions, your context and your pupils. Even more, I want to provoke you into challenging yourself to be that little bit better, that little bit more ninja.

VOCABULARY ISN'T A LESSON, IT'S LIFE

Before we discuss the problem, let's look at the solution: **vocabulary isn't a lesson, it's life**. We can't think about timetabling it or giving it a slot in which it can be observed. Due to the hectic nature of teaching, we find a strange comfort in being able to box something up, put it in a slot, so that we can tick it off, say it's done, forget about it for today. The safety net has been cast…

So, the solution. The solution is valuing every interaction, every conversation, every minute, every hour, every lesson and every day. Each smaller moment enhances the next. If we value all of the smaller parts of learning, the larger parts will take care of themselves. When I talk about being a 'Vocabulary Ninja', albeit a little corny, this is what I mean: being present in each and every moment as a class teacher and understanding that vocabulary and language are constants, that they permeate every aspect of life, both in and out of school. Being present is one thing, but we must be vigilant and ready to act, model, prepare, discuss, correct, celebrate, joke and inspire, too. There is simply no way that we can compartmentalise it, contain it, box it up, timetable it, say 'it's done'. You have to be ready to pounce on every opportunity. And believe me, there will be lots of opportunities, because there are lots of words!

BECOME A VOCABULARY NINJA GRAND MASTER

As a teacher myself, I used to find comfort in knowing something had been 'developed or produced' to meet the needs of a certain year, a word list for example, or a specific text and planned unit. As time has passed, I have found that this comfort blanket didn't really help me. Instead, it insulated me from that fear factor and gave me something to blame if things didn't go quite right. By fear factor, bluntly, I mean that such subject packs insulated me from poor levels of subject knowledge, my area of weakness. Actually, I just needed to take responsibility and become better at what I did.

I needed to understand words in much more detail because they made up every aspect of what I taught – the grammar, the etymology, the conventions, the terminology, everything do with it. I had to make myself a better teacher before I stood a chance of developing more successful and confident pupils. This is still true today. Each day I try to be micro-ambitious and aim to be marginally better by the end of it.

WORD DEPRIVATION

From a solution to a problem. What is 'word deprivation'? Quite simply, word deprivation is a lack of words that a learner can draw upon in written and oral communication. In other words, they have a limited vocabulary. On the other hand, pupils with more expansive and broad repertoires of words could be thought of as being 'word-rich'. Alex Quigley, author of *Closing the Vocabulary Gap*, refers to this concept as pupils being 'word-wealthy', whereby pupils need to develop a vocabulary of 50,000 words if they are statistically likely to be successful in education and beyond. This is a huge undertaking when you consider that 'average' pupils learn 2,000–3,000 words a year in education. Whichever way you look at it, the curriculum alone and general teaching is not sufficient for most pupils to reach this magical figure for working vocabulary. Let's not forget, these are the figures for the average pupil;. What about those pupils who have other significant barriers to learning – your pupil premium, special education needs, socially mobile, English as an additional language and so on? You can see how, quite quickly, a large number of pupils are likely to be word-deprived – literally starved of words, consumed by a lexical famine.

If pupils don't understand enough words (not the elaborate and fancy ones – I mean the ones we take for granted and assume that pupils know), how can we expect them to engage at any level within the classroom? Let's think back to how vocabulary can be a barrier to learning. For some pupils, even in the early stages of school, the barriers are huge and sadly misunderstood. Educators may spot that there is an issue, but a pupil's working lexical level probably isn't the first thing most educators will think about investigating. Thus, the curriculum moves on and the barrier becomes bigger and harder to overcome. Yes, this won't always be the case for certain pupils; some children have additional barriers that impact on learning. But if we focus on the majority of pupils, we can ensure that pupils are actively expanding their vocabularies, making regular deposits to their 'word bank' and becoming word-hungry, rather than starved of words. This is our responsibility and one that, if we can tackle it, will have far-reaching effects – across subjects, schools and all pupils' journey in life.

THE NATIONAL CURRICULUM

The National Curriculum lists 100 spellings for Years 5 and 6. Two whole years of learning, restricted to 100 'essential' words that are found as requirements for national writing expectations, display boards and beyond. There are millions of words for us to explore, so why do we restrict ourselves? We have to aspire to be better, more adventurous and drag ourselves away from this safety net approach to words and vocabulary.

The Oxford Living Dictionaries estimates there are somewhere in the region of three quarters of a million words in the English language and, as stated earlier, pupils require a working vocabulary of 50,000 words. Yet somehow we are happy to accept that just 100 of those words are a vital component of two whole years of school. I find this hard to accept or endorse. It's a huge contradiction and one that we must be aware of for the best interests of our pupils. Now, let's be clear: I am not trying to rain down some form of anarchistic vocabulary-based rebellion against the National Curriculum. Far from it. But deciding that only 0.013 per cent of all the possible words available to us should be deemed an essential focus over two years just seems insane. Let's bring in another analogy. Let's compare our 'word-diet' with an actual diet: if you were to consume only 0.013 per cent of the available food sources over a two-year period, regardless of what they were, you would be most likely in a state of great ill-health, dangerously malnourished or, most likely, not be here to read this fabulous book. You would have been deprived of the crucial vitamins,

minerals, proteins and nutrients of a balanced diet that are essential for good health. Well, the same applies if we want to be 'word healthy'. We need to consume a balanced diet of words from a range of sources and contexts:

- high-quality texts
- conversation
- independent reading
- being read to
- modelled writing
- listening to others
- non-fiction and fiction
- poetry
- direct teaching
- books
- picture books
- assemblies
- trips and experts
- break times
- performances.

This isn't an exhaustive list either – the opportunities are endless; words and language can be drawn from anywhere. If we are to promote more creative, inquisitive and independent learners, we need to be a little bit more, well, ninja, and pounce on every one of the opportunities alluded to above. This will ultimately help make children better readers, writers and communicators.

ARE TEACHERS THE PROBLEM?

So, hopefully we agree that we need an enriched diet of language. But, are teachers one of the problems when it comes to word deprivation? I think I was, so maybe we are. Due to the complex nature of teaching, it would be fair to moot that vocabulary is something that we hope happens. For some of us, thinking about the nuts and bolts of words and language is just something that we don't have time for, or don't realise the importance of. Teaching is undoubtedly one of the most rewarding, yet challenging, professions; some of us even see teaching as their *raison d'être*, their 'reason for being'. Even the process of becoming a teacher, whichever route taken, involves late nights, early mornings, blood, sweat, tears, and the unpredictable on a daily basis. We are so exhaustingly busy, working in this high-pressure environment that the system creates, that it is easy to lose focus on what's important. My point is that words are what are important, and that we have potentially lost sight of this fundamental fact. Words can be the biggest barriers to learning for pupils but are also the most powerful weapons we could hope to equip them with.

Let's refocus and think about 'word deprivation'. If our pupils have a limited understanding of words, then pronouncing, reading, writing, sharing, choosing, playing with words all become increasingly difficult. These basic skills that begin in Reception become barriers to learning because words help to form nearly every aspect of the curriculum that a child is exposed to, in some way, shape or form. Yet, I think pupils, NQTs and experienced teachers alike have been done a huge disservice, for a long time, in being made to believe that words, vocabulary and language will just be learnt and understood on their own. Again, we come back to a safety net approach to teaching, where security for teachers is found in word banks, lists, schemes and being told what to do so that we don't get in 'trouble'. And this is understandable – believe me, I get it – but we need to just get over this and start to be braver.

We must start to think for ourselves, be brave, make decisions, be passionate and get excited. Be more ninja. I understand that your school will have systems and processes that teachers will need to adhere to, but within all of that noise, you just have to find your inner Vocabulary Ninja.

USING THE IDEAS IN THIS BOOK

As discussed earlier, being a little bit more ninja doesn't mean you are going to begin to teach your own rebellious curriculum. It means you are going to increase the value of every idle opportunity or lazy expression that the day offers up. Let's look at a typical day:

You have a guided reading session to teach first, then have to lead an assembly before introducing a new mathematical concept and, in English, you must edit those final drafts just before lunch. This will involve devouring a pork pie and rice as you set-up for PE and resource your geography lesson for last period. Oh and you're on break duty too. Your TA is off sick and the office staff have kindly informed you that the photocopier is broken. Awesome!

Within all of this mayhem that is teaching, your ninja mentality and focus on vocabulary is vital. What is it that's important? As you can already see, there is no extra time in your day to dedicate to vocabulary. Vocabulary and words will encompass all of these events and the pockets of time within and between every lesson. This is where you will make the difference; this is where you need to go it alone and take control.

There is a level of genuine and pure exhilaration that comes from taking control, believe me, it's great. Yes, undoubtedly mistakes will be made, but at least they are yours; at least you can feel an emotion, such as regret. Even in experiencing regret, there is still

satisfaction in knowing that you *tried*. I don't really think anyone ever really learned from someone else's mistakes. You have to experience it yourself. What makes it yet more powerful is when you quickly start to reap the rewards, as you will when your pupils begin to use this language in conversations and in their writing.

To begin with, it's quite simply all about having the right mentality.

THREE MANTRAS

Mantras can often offer up insights into the type of mindset we are trying to adopt. Again, this isn't about rebellion, it's about belief and positivity – you can do it, you are amazing. Here are three mantras that Vocabulary Ninja loves, all with varying levels of formality – but nonetheless powerful and apt. Plus, every ninja needs a mantra, it's a ninja thing.

'YOU GOTTA BACK YOURSELF!'

Certainly the most informal example of the three, but it's great. 'You gotta back yourself!' is so true. Everything in the last five to six paragraphs could have just been edited out and this mantra put in its place. Sport has messages and principles that adapt extremely easily into education – marginal gains, for example. For me, 'you gotta back yourself' was a mantra that came to life while studying and playing sport competitively at the University of Hull. It was often used in jest between myself and housemates, Mr Sims, Mr Rodley, Mr Grant, Mr Jackson and Mr Kench (whose names I use so formally as all are now teachers too, not the cast list of Reservoir Dogs!). You have to back yourself. The classroom is your domain, so make decisions and see them through, reflect and go again.

'IT'S BETTER TO ASK FOR FORGIVENESS THAN TO ASK FOR PERMISSION'

The next mantra is most likely a headteacher's worst nightmare come to fruition, but let's not worry about that too much. Believe in yourself – if you have an idea, it's probably a good one, so go for it. Sometimes there is a level of security in asking for permission. It absolves you of responsibility. You are far more likely to invest yourself in something if it is your idea, your project, and if you are personally invested in the outcomes. This is a great position to be in. I'm not for one minute suggesting you all of a sudden take a group of children on an unannounced trip to your nearest dangerous place. No. I want you to think about your classroom, corridors, nooks, crannies, spaces, unused equipment, facilities, routines and so on. Be creative and forward thinking. Be inventive. Tear down that display; take apart a monitor; do the latest Twitter-trending edu-idea; be passionate. Just do it! You, your pupils and your school will reap the rewards.

Unless we are prepared to take control of our classroom, our own practice and what we prioritise, then (as a famous film once said) resistance is futile. Once you have the right mindset, you can begin your own journey towards developing yourself, driving your CPD in the direction you want it to be driven, and knowing that you are making decisions for you and your learners!

'DON'T CELEBRATE TOO PROFUSELY IN VICTORY OR BERATE YOURSELF TOO MUCH IN DEFEAT'

The final mantra that resonates from personal experiences throughout my time in education is this: 'don't celebrate too profusely in victory or berate yourself too much in defeat'. Victory and defeat could also be re-worded as highs and lows, or ups and downs. The essence of this mantra is all about maintaining a grasp on level headedness or perspective. No matter how good you think you are, you can get better, and if things seem bad, they're probably not as bad as you think. The parallels to sport are easy to see once again. Listen to any professional sports person or team interviewed after a euphoric win or demoralising defeat. In that moment, they will be overjoyed with happiness or overcome with grief, but it is the most successful amongst them who manage to move on very quickly and learn from what has taken place – whether it was positive or negative. Yes, celebrate, or be disappointed, but learn quickly and move on. Tomorrow is another day to strive to improve from where we are now.

VOCABULARY AND YOU

So what do mentalities and mantras have to do with mastering vocabulary? Well, everything really. Just as it has everything to do with education and everything to do with you. There is never one without the other; each is a vital component, reliant on the other. We all have good and bad days, and the same can be said for lessons, conversations, lesson plans, observations, or even whole years. Part of my own journey in understanding the importance of vocabulary was more of a journey in understanding myself and not listening to too many external influences, and doing each day on my terms. So in one sense, it was more like a journey to believing in myself rather than just believing in vocabulary. Vocabulary became my unwitting partner and passion!

Once again, we must bring ourselves back to word deprivation. Without making words a priority, the children in your class will always be deprived of

words or be falling well short of the magical 50,000. Prioritising words will open up the doors to a whole new world of understanding for you and your pupils. You need to be your class's Vocabulary Ninja. You need to back yourself. You may need to ask for forgiveness, in victory or defeat, but be content in knowing that you will have made a much bigger difference than you can ever comprehend.

THE MOST PRECIOUS COMMODITY

The world is forever changing, becoming smaller, and at an exponential rate over the last 20 years due to technology, politics, economics and social norms changing beyond recognition. It's hard to keep up. The world is a very fast-moving place now for young people to be; technology has rapidly become virtually indispensable for everyone. Video games, smartphones, apps, social media, virtual reality and television are developed and consumed at a mind-boggling rate. There are so many fabulous innovations and advances that make the world a more exciting place to live. All the while, people and families are becoming increasingly busy, and even with all of these technological conveniences, time is still the most precious commodity. And that is why what you do with your pupils during the short time you spend with them is critical.

For just a moment, let's forget financial poverty and political climates, and think carefully about our pupils living in 'word poverty'. When we think about word poverty, it's important to think about all pupils, not just pupils who may be living in actual poverty. Word poverty is all about time and exposure. How much of our pupils' time involves exposure to high-quality language, words and vocabulary? Pupils will always spend significantly more time at home or in environments other than school. It's during these times that individual experiences and exposure to language will vary dramatically. Some pupils will read daily, be read to and have diverse conversations filled with expressive language with adults who have robust vocabularies of their own. Lots of children won't have this experience.

The pupils in your care might only be exposed to your enriched environment for 30 of 168 hours in a week. That's only 17 per cent of every week that is spent in a language-rich and hopefully word-wealthy environment where words are celebrated, played with and valued. Take away break times, lunchtimes, assemblies, days off and trips, and it's probably closer to 15 per cent of every week. Each year, of the 8,760 hours in that year, it's likely that a pupil will spend no more than 1,140 hours with you – that's 13 per cent of that whole year! Why not break it down even further? Of those six hours in school each day, if you only ever focused on words for an English or reading lesson, let's say five hours a week for example, you would only be actively engaging in 'language' for three per cent of a seven-day week or two per cent of every year, which, scarily enough, equates to 55.1 school days spent focusing on 'language' during a pupil's time from Reception to Year 6.

Make time for vocabulary each day. Just five to 15 minutes. You won't regret it.

We can't create more time, and the curriculum is demanding. Go back to the principles of being a Vocabulary Ninja. Every interaction, every conversation, every minute, every lesson, every day is vital – it's about the sum of all the small parts and valuing the marginal gains of each interaction, taking pride in the micro-victories and evaluating your micro-defeats. We have to make the most of the time that pupils are with us in school.

What is mind blowing about numbers like these is that, considering how little time might actually be spent on 'language' in the grand scheme, you do an amazing job in the short space of time that you actually have with your pupils. Vivid and heart-breaking narratives, emotive poetry, captivating diary entries and forensic non-fiction reports – it's all magnificent.

Some pupils, in fact a large proportion of pupils, will spend a much larger percentage of time doing things other than being exposed to high-quality language. And believe it or not, this is OK. We want children to live exciting lives out in the world, kicking balls, climbing trees, gaming, having sleepovers and so on. But, not everyone lives in this idealistic land of childhood.

This raises two very important issues to be aware of. One is that the time that pupils spend with you in school is extremely precious, more valuable than you previously realised. Every interaction, every conversation, every minute, every hour, every day is unspeakably valuable. Two, language and vocabulary must be at the centre of everything that we do in every aspect of the school day; confining it to one lesson just isn't good enough.

'THE ANIMALS THAT USE THE POND DON'T JUST DRINK FROM IT'

You know better than most that, depending on their context, some of your pupils will be exposed to some pretty terrible vocabulary on a daily basis. The word pool that they swim in every day is extremely shallow, it doesn't rain very often and lots of the animals that use the pond don't just drink from it. People will generally only use the vocabulary that their environment demands of them, meaning that the interactions your pupils have on a daily basis – the people who surround them, the jobs their parents do and so on – directly affects the vocabulary they will subconsciously use. Your job is to begin to make this a conscious process. As alluded to earlier, the time spent with you is indescribably valuable.

You need to bring the rain! Not in the military sense, but in the climatological sense. You need to be the cumulonimbus cloud that pours down onto your pupils' shallow word pool, making it a little deeper in each moment and understanding that every raindrop matters. Even now, I'm especially careful not to say *each day*, and I'll say it once again – *every* interaction, *every* conversation, *every* minute, *every* hour will make up every day. Thinking about each day is too big, it isn't micro-ambitious enough, it allows for gaps, missed opportunities. If we are micro-ambitious enough and understand the importance of every raindrop, we will begin to turn our shallow vocabulary puddles into vast reservoirs of language.

BECOMING A VOCABULARY NINJA

Anecdotes, metaphors, myths and analogies aside, I can only presume that you would like to know a little more about the impact vocabulary can have within the classroom and why you should be a Vocabulary Ninja.

As stated earlier, vocabulary cuts across all aspects of your curriculum. Being micro-ambitious with vocabulary and focusing at a word level can have a profound effect on pupils' writing. The great thing about vocabulary is that it is extremely accessible for all pupils – it literally empowers them, they can control it and it's theirs. By bringing vocabulary to the forefront of your teaching, using the strategies identified in the book, you will quickly begin to improve writing standards across the curriculum because of the wider vocabulary and increased understanding of pupils. Pupils will quickly become adept at using more complex language, varying verbs and adjectives, while developing a greater capacity to show and not tell (offering inference via vocabulary to the audience). Quite quickly, 'big' will become 'enormous'; 'happy' will become 'elated'; and what was once 'boring' will become 'mundane', even 'tedious'. Repetition of language will reduce and pupils' shallow word pools will have become a little deeper.

A word of warning: as with all learning, not all pupils will necessarily be ready to work at the same word level. Success, progress, achievement – whatever you want to call it – will present itself in very different ways for different pupils. You should value and celebrate them equally. This phrase perfectly encapsulates this sentiment: 'One child's "*huge*" is another child's "*voracious*".' (Jack Phillips, @Mr_P_Hillips, describing two very different pupils, both increasing their word pool depth and becoming increasingly word wealthy). Both word choices are just as fantastic and wonderful as the other. They are both filled with authorial intent, unique voices and an empowered independence. The impact of vocabulary on pupil writing is potentially endless, only limited by the words they are limited to. (I just blew my own mind!)

A WORD ABOUT GRAMMAR

A word-level focus within writing also offers perpetual opportunities to embed discussion linked to the basics of grammar. Every word has a job. Within every sentence, each word is performing a role, and, as you know, some words are rather versatile and can perform many different jobs. Grammar is another area where you find the teaching safety net, mostly because of a 'requires improvement' level of subject knowledge. The teaching of grammar becomes an endless list of clichés or phrases that are competently repeated by pupils. You know the ones: 'adjectives are describing words', 'verbs are doing words' and 'a noun is a person place or a thing'. You hear these safety net phrases all of the time – we find comfort in them. I used to say them regularly, mostly because I wasn't confident in my subject knowledge or even with the basics of grammar. The problem with all of these phrases is that they are all superficial. There is no depth of knowledge or understanding for either the teacher or the learner. It's all just smoke and mirrors!

The scenario probably goes a little like this: during an English observation, grammar inevitably crops up. With the observer hovering closely over your shoulder or while keenly inspecting your displays, you are busy working with Jimmy and his table of typical pupils. You are helping them develop a descriptive passage about an engaging Literacy Shed video. You decide that adding some adjectives is the next step (as per the plan). You ask the table, 'Who can give me an adjective to make this sentence a little more impressive?' Only to be greeted by blank expressions (not per the plan). In your head, you are furious: 'I can't believe they are doing this to me! We did it yesterday! Aaarggggghhhh!' You wisely decide to widen the discussion. You offer up the usual question, 'Can somebody tell me what an adjective is?' Hands from the usual suspects rise and the inevitable answer will come, 'It's a describing

word, sir.' You graciously accept the answer, with a nod to the observer and move on, satisfied that you have demonstrated your subject knowledge, even though your focus group and the wider class is probably still none the wiser.

In order for grammatical understanding to improve for teacher and learners, we must begin to develop a more open culture where each new word offers an opportunity for grammatical discussion. We need to be more forensic in our approach to each word that we encounter. The brilliant thing about discussing grammar while discussing words is that it offers up context, making any discussions and learning more memorable. Some of the most memorable contexts will undoubtedly come from the books that you are reading in class. This is why exposure to high-quality literature is so important. Subsequent chapters will provide glossaries, agreed terminology, activities and strategies to improve the teaching and learning of grammar in your classroom.

WHERE TO FIND INSPIRATION AND SUPPORT

Literacy, reading, writing, grammar, spelling and vocabulary are all inextricably (awesome word meaning 'impossible to disentangle or separate') linked – no one area is more important than any other; the success of one stems from another. Developing your ninja mentality and a forensic classroom culture are essential if your pupils are to learn. Your journey towards a ninja mentality and forensic classroom culture will allow you to be fully engaged with every learning moment that words present.

Ultimately, I want to convince you that making vocabulary a priority is worthwhile and to provoke you into thinking about how you can improve. Undoubtedly there will be significant barriers. Will those barriers go away? Probably not. So it will be tough, that's for sure. Definitely use research to support what you do, seek the support of other professionals, and read a journal or become active on Twitter. (Personally, I'd suggest the latter!) If you do decide to dive into the world of #EduTwitter, opposite are a few accounts that you should think about following and some of the hashtags to use while tweeting, to connect with the vast education community based on Twitter.

NINJA NOTES

Follow @TheTeacherTrain and @MrMCGrammar on Twitter for some of the most inspirational grammar resources and teaching techniques!

PEOPLE TO FOLLOW

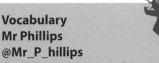

Vocabulary
Mr Phillips
@Mr_P_hillips
A teacher passionate about vocabulary, language and books. A true advocate of the word. Constantly sharing ideas and good practice. Creator and curator of 'The Word Gang'.

Writing
Tim Roach
@MrTRoach
Tim is a Year 6 teacher and English leader. Tim is a genuine lover of books and promoter of teaching ideas for primary English and grammar.

Books and reading
Paul Watson
@PaulWat4
Passionate about books for education. Blogger. Curator of The Great British Book Worm blog. Regular reviews and recommendations.

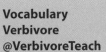

Vocabulary
Verbivore
@VerbivoreTeach
A devourer of words and consumer of language. Another fabulous collection of vocabulary resources, ideas and pedagogy. A real must for any pedagogical arsenal.

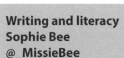

Writing and literacy
Sophie Bee
@_MissieBee
Teacher, blogger and English lead. Self-professed grammar pedant and number nerd. Sophie offers high quality teaching discussion, resources and analysis!

Books and reading
Simon Smith
@smithsmm
Headteacher, mad about books! He is a real advocate of picture books and the stories that they can tell. Books, books, books and more books!

Vocabulary
Alex Quigley
@HuntingEnglish
English teacher, Associate at Education Endowment Foundation and author of 'Closing the Vocabulary Gap'. A modern authority on vocabulary research.

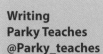

Writing
Parky Teaches
@Parky_teaches
A KS2 teacher, blogger, writing ambassador and creator of the Pens of Calligra @LostPens. Inspirer of writing in the classroom.

Books and reading
Caroline Ash
@cazzash
Deputy Headteacher, passionate about books and the role that they play in school. Also promotes @WomensEd and gender equality via @gendercharter.

Vocabulary
Robert Macfarlane
@RobGMacfarlane
Author of 'The Lost Words' and wordsmith. Rob shares intriguing language on a regular basis.

SPaG and GaPS
Mr. M
@TheTeacherTrain
One of the most creative, exciting and inspirational teachers in education. Creator of MC Grammar and Resilient Reader – Legends of Literacy Creator.

Books and reading
Ashley Booth
@MrBoothY6
Y6 teacher, maths, reading and computing lead. Loves maths reasoning & children's literature. Literacy Shed Plus writer.

General teaching inspiration (not exhaustive)

Chris Dyson, @chrisdysonHT
Graham Andre, @grahamandre
Miss Khan, @MissKhan__
Miss Merrill, @MissSMerrill
Ed Finch, @MrEFinch
Colin Grimes, @MrGPrimary
David Keyte, @Mr_K_Teacher
Sam Keys, @mr_k3ys
Primary Rocks, @PrimaryRocks1
Rob Smith, @redgierob
Teacher Glitter, @Teacherglitter
Aiden Severs, @thatboycanteach
Mike Watson, @WatsEd

#Hashtags to use

#PrimaryRocks
#EduTwitter
#ReadingRocks
#BrewEd
#TheGoldenH
#EdTech
#EdChat
#Teacher

TWITTER EVIDENCE FOR THE VOCABULARY NINJA APPROACH

Research studies and evidence have become a core part of research-based education theory. You can find out what research says about a programme, which programmes have high impact vs cost, which interventions work best, the effectiveness of TAs and so on. Research is great and I suppose evidence is even better.

More often than not when it comes to resources, teachers want to know if something has impact, engages pupils and is easy to deliver. Vocabulary Ninja is all three. The brilliance of Twitter has meant that Vocabulary Ninja has had an impact across the globe already. I can only apologise for the lack of opinions from boffins – only teachers here, being ninja every day. Here are just a few snippets of the feedback the Vocabulary Ninja approach receives on a regular basis. The best thing about collecting feedback via social media is that it creates a shared community that everyone can draw upon. Have a look and then take the principles of being a Vocabulary Ninja and adapt them for yourself, your context and your pupils.

Rosemary Burke
@Rosemarycalm

Child 'We were waiting for the bus. It was taking too long so I said to mum waiting is tedious.' @VocabularyNinja

6 Sep 2017

Joanne Throssell
@jct72hkr

@VocabularyNinja It's working writing speech between monster & boy and found 'infernal' & 'hellish' in there. I didn't ask or remind.

6 Sep 2017

Colin Grimes
@MrGPrimary

The power you have in my classroom. Kids on the playground asking what the ninja word was today!

9 Oct 2017

Chris Jacques
@MrCJ248

The Ninja is working hard in our class. @VocabularyNinja

1 Mar 2018

Miss Verny
@SomersPark4NV

It is #inevitable 4NV use #copious words of the day while writing. Endless #possibilities to include #unpredictable vocabulary, without #grimacing. You may even say they do so #nonchalantly. They #anticipate it eagerly and are #fastidious in their application. @VocabularyNinja

13 Nov 2018

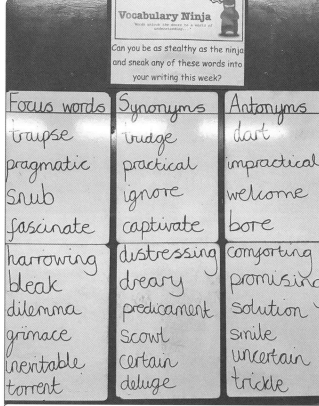

Miss H
@Miss_SH_teacher

Taking up only a small space of a cupboard door - one of the simplest but most powerful and well-used displays in my classroom. We love our daily @VocabularyNinja words. Today's "torrent, deluge, trickle" words will crop up in this week's sea poetry I'm sure! @HCPScolchester

13 Nov 2018

This small snapshot of 'impact' comes from real classrooms, real pupils and real teachers who are overcoming real barriers. The impact is real; it isn't reported about in a renowned scientific journal, forgotten about in some dusty room or filed neatly in an archive. It is alive, it's breathing, every single day, all across the world! This is something that Vocabulary Ninja is incredibly proud of, and the sentiments of teachers like @MrGPrimary (aka Colin Grimes, former soldier and currently a class teacher from Rothbury, in Northumberland) are the only peer reviews I will ever value!

But before any of that will truly make a difference, you have to be ready to make a change and become a little bit more ninja. I know you can do it. I believe in you already!

NINJA NOTES

Don't be too proud. Try out ideas from Twitter in your own classroom.

3 – TAUGHT VS ENCOUNTERED VOCABULARY

Believe it or not, discussion around taught vs encountered vocabulary can often turn into heated debate. It's the classic traditional vs progressive teaching debate, or a little bit like the great, enduring cream tea debate. Cream tea has been served in the UK since the 11th century and people have ruminated on the order of spreading the scone's traditional toppings ever since. While those in Devon typically spread the clotted cream first followed by jam, the Cornish tradition is to spread jam first followed by cream. Decisions, decisions… but, ultimately, who cares? Scones, cream and jam are awesome! All three parts are just as equally important and, quite frankly, delicious. So we can sit around debating which way is better, or we could get stuck in and just eat some scones. I know which I'll be doing *says while wiping away jammy, creamy crumbs*.

Next time you have a scone, tweet me a picture! #ninjascone

I guess I'm trying to say that the process of eating and enjoying the scones is way more important than debating which type is better, when considering all of the constituent parts are the same. Flipping the context back to vocabulary: if we can appreciate that taught and encountered vocabulary can both offer valuable teaching opportunities, then we are in a much stronger position to increase the word wealth of our pupils.

TAUGHT VOCABULARY

Let's start to think about what taught vocabulary is and its importance within the classroom. Taught vocabulary encompasses an in-detail, planned approach to vocabulary, where you will 'teach' your pupils about a specific word, all of its associations and all that it encompasses. Planning for the teaching of specific vocabulary is crucial; you can't just rely on high-quality and relevant vocabulary to reveal itself at the moment you require it. Plus, if we rely on chance,

we will always be in deficit of our 50,000 words target for our working vocabularies.

We know we only have a short time with our learners over their time in primary education, even less in secondary, so ensuring we have a clear rationale as to the words we are choosing to expose pupils to is crucial. We can't afford to waste these opportunities. Here are four relevant rationales for teaching vocabulary:

- widening and deepening pupils' vocabulary pools
- targeted teaching of rich vocabulary for writing
- pre-teaching for reading
- general understanding of vocabulary.

WIDENING AND DEEPENING PUPILS' VOCABULARY POOLS

In the first instance, we may just be aiming to widen a pupil's vocabulary. For example, we might decide to select a word that could act as both a noun and a verb depending on how it is used within a certain sentence. This type of word is extremely useful. It might also be that a word has multiple modifications in terms of prefixes, suffixes, synonyms and antonyms. So by teaching just one word, we are actually exposing a learner to 10-15 other associated words and modifications! The more associations pupils can make with words, the more likely they are to retain this new learning. This is why word choice is so important in the first instance. See the 'Chain' meaning tree, opposite, for an example of what I mean.

Some words may have very few other associations and you might hit a dead end very quickly if you haven't carefully thought about your planned vocabulary opportunities. But, just because a word doesn't have 15+ modifications, doesn't mean it is any less important or valuable in the context you hope it will be used. As a professional, you will need to make this judgement call.

Subject knowledge at this point is a crucial element that will impact on your ability to expertly explain all of the important elements of these specifically chosen words. Do your homework and ensure you understand the morphology of the words you're teaching. For example, you should be up to speed on how tense affects the chosen words and which prefixes can be used with it.

'CHAIN' MEANING TREE

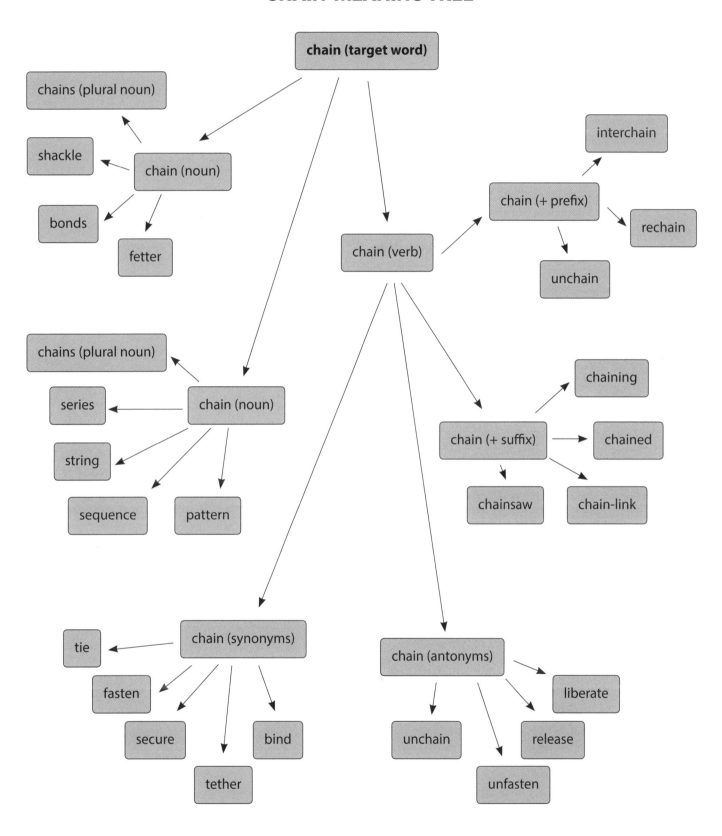

To be confident about teaching a bespoke word each day, a comprehensive subject knowledge and understanding of terminology is essential. Master the basics of your subject knowledge and you will be ready to incorporate taught vocabulary into your teaching practice. The elements suggested below are the most common grammatical areas that will arise when teaching new vocabulary to children. You should be confident in discussing and using them. As suggested earlier, within the taught element of vocabulary, you can plan carefully for the spelling, punctuation and grammar of each word.

You should be confident in discussing and using grammatical terms with your class. At the most basic level, you should understand the following terms and how they apply to any word you are teaching: noun, verb, adjective, determiner, synonym, antonym, suffix, prefix.

THE WORD PLAN

It's probably the perfect time to discuss Vocabulary Ninja's plans for world domination! Errrm, sorry, that's a different book. I meant plans for *word* domination. That's right – my word plan. As alluded to earlier, having a sound subject knowledge is crucial in allowing you to flow with discussions and teaching that encountering vocabulary will undoubtedly present. In the first instance, it's a great idea to plan out your knowledge of a word. The word plan isn't necessarily a lesson plan; it's designed to arrange your subject knowledge of the word, ready to discuss with pupils.

Let's make it clear from the outset: Vocabulary Ninja is fully aware of the demands on a modern teacher's time (believe me, I know!). I'm not for one minute advocating that you need to plan for every word that you intend to teach, but it might be useful to organise your word knowledge and child-friendly definitions. Sometimes using a 'new' word in a child-friendly manner can stump even the most knowledgeable teacher but with the word plan, five minutes, a prudent scribble here and there, you're done. You will become increasingly confident with common vocabulary. The word plan will then evolve as a practical tool, where it may be used to explore more challenging vocabulary before it is exposed to pupils, ensuring synonyms are relevant or that you

have an example prepared within a multi-clause sentence so that you incorporate SPaG elements into your teaching. Remember: if the objective is to widen pupils' vocabulary, then we must choose words that are going to serve that purpose and meet that objective. Spending 15 minutes on the word 'caravan', a noun, won't offer up much other vocabulary. As a noun, it is what it is – a caravan.

On the next page is an example of how you might complete the word plan document to organise your word knowledge.

TARGETED TEACHING OF MEANING-RICH VOCABULARY FOR WRITING

Widening and deepening a pupil's vocabulary has to be an ongoing and conscious part of your daily teaching – adding to your pupil's pool each and every day. The widening of their vocabulary is a very broad objective, a splattering of vocabulary if you will. Much like launching a rock that you can barely carry into a pond, it's going to make a big splash. Everyone and everything in its vicinity are going to be moistened, to a greater or lesser degree. Sometimes, though, we might need to be a little more precise with the outcomes we hope to achieve. So, as opposed to widening general vocabulary (which must of course remain a focus), we need depth. In other words, we need to teach a specific word for its rich nature and target its use within writing.

As a professional educator (although I'm not sure there's such a thing as an amateur educator), we can safely assume that you will have a wider and deeper social, academic and literary vocabulary to draw upon than your pupils. Using this vast knowledge of language, and incorporating some of the wonderful resources available to you on the internet and in books, you can teach some very specific meaning-rich words to your pupils. These targeted, meaning-rich words will be chosen by you in the knowledge that they can be used in the very near future, that day even, in a pupil's writing. These words will often be extremely powerful and help the author (your pupil) elicit emotion from the audience as they read. They are those words that help an author *show* what is happening in their work, rather than simply *telling* the reader.

Contextualised examples – Context is crucial for vocabulary learning. Depending on the context that you are talking or writing about, certain associations and modifications will be more or less appropriate for use. From the 'chain' example, one word that hasn't been noted as a synonym is 'moor'. Moor wasn't included in the list of synonyms due to its specific relevance to the context of the ocean and harbours, i.e. 'the boat was moored'. We wouldn't want to use 'moor' as a straight swap for the verb 'chain' in most contexts. Context is crucial.

WORD PLAN

Vocabulary Ninja © Andrew Jennings, 2019

Target word:	chain	Text reference:	*A Christmas Carol*, page 23
Word class:	verb, noun	Pronunciation:	*chain*
Definition:	Noun: A chain is a series of metal hoops that are linked together. Verb: To chain means to attach one thing to another.		
Contextualised examples:	Noun example: Vocabulary Ninja always ensured he used **a chain** to secure his bicycle. Verb example: It is essential **to chain** your bike to a fence before going inside a shop.		

Synonyms:	Antonyms:	Prefixes:	Suffixes:	Rhyming words:
Noun: bonds, shackles Verb: tie, fasten, secure, tether, bind	Verb: unchain, unfasten, release, liberate	unchain, rechain, interchain	chained, chaining	pain, plain, brain, plane, rain, stain, grain

24

Synonyms and antonyms – These are associations of the word. When I refer to associations, I am typically referring to synonyms and antonyms, as well as variations to nouns. They are words that might be directly or maybe even tenuously linked to the target word. In the 'chain' example, there are 16 words that we might consider as having association (not all of them are included here).

Prefixes and suffixes – These are modifications. Generally, the root of the word remains constant with various prefixes and suffixes being added to modify the word and its meaning. Within the 'chain' example there are five examples of modifications. Yet again, the list of modifications provided isn't exhaustive and some more obscure modifications are possible to find.

WORD PLAN

Target word:		Text reference:
Word class:		Pronunciation:
Definition:		
Contextualised examples:		

Synonyms:	Antonyms:	Prefixes:	Suffixes:	Rhyming words:

These meaning-rich words will mostly likely have very few prefixes or suffixes, and in most instances have no 'context appropriate' synonyms or antonyms – very low association and modification value. Such words don't widen a pupil's general vocabulary, but remember: that's not what we are aiming to achieve by teaching these words. By teaching meaning-rich words, we will add *depth* to our word pool. Power now comes from precision, not the splattering as before. This time, the rock you have chosen has a precise shape, an evenly distributed weight and a smooth texture, perfect for the job you have chosen it for – skimming. When you choose the perfect stone for skimming, the onlookers are entranced as your stone bounces elegantly time after time across the still surface of the water; the same applies to word choice. Enabling pupils to make meaningful and evocative word choices can have a profound effect on the audience. First, we need to facilitate the deepening of word knowledge for pupils to draw upon with independence and purpose.

NINJA NOTES

Put an A4 piece of paper with 'prefix' written on it to the left of your whiteboard and an A4 piece of paper with 'suffix' to the right. Refer to these when you're teaching a new word.

There isn't any significant difference to the manner in which we would approach a meaning-rich word compared to a more common word. The word plan will still be a useful document for organising your ideas, and relevant contextual examples will be so, so important to ensuring that the children understand the word. In a lot of instances, meaning-rich words will take the form of an adjective or a verb, so having some pertinent images to support your contextual example will help bring the word to life for your learners. Crucially, during this discreet teaching time, giving pupils the opportunity to use the word within a written sentence of their own is essential. This helps embed the word within their own chosen context and also gives less confident writers a practical example of their own to draw upon at a later date. I will refer to this whole teaching process in detail in subsequent chapters.

One of the greatest things about meaning-rich words is that '*real*' authors also use them in the children's literature that they write. Pupils who read independently will encounter them on a page-by-page basis, which is fabulous. However, for younger pupils, the less confident and the reluctant readers in your class, you will need to be the fountain from which those words flow through the books you expose them to. For children, giving them the power to use something that an actual author uses in their book is immeasurably valuable. Why? Because children mimic everything that they are exposed to – monkey see, monkey do. Why wouldn't the same be true for vocabulary? The more often learners are exposed to high-quality language, and the more often they are given the opportunity to use it, the more likely it is that this language will become part of the person that they are.

Meaning-rich words for young children

At a very young age – in EYFS and KS1 – meaning-rich words can be very simple and are progressive. They could be colours and shades, names of seaside objects, insects and so on. Children at this age are learning at an unprecedented rate and absorbing everything that they experience; they will never again learn at this rate in their lives. This is where their conscious word journey must begin. Miss it and we all miss out.

NINJA NOTES

Make EYFS and KS1 word-rich environments too. Get labelling!

Building word wealth at this early age is essential, so that understanding from listening to real sources of communication (video, teaching, discussion) or from written sources (books, texts, worksheets) becomes second nature and not a barrier to learning, as it can be. Let's think about our pupils with 'behaviour issues' and let's just be really honest. Why do they present like this? Well, because in most instances, they can't read well enough to access what you present them with. OK, OK, I can hear you. Of course there are children that will have other barriers to learning that you will need to navigate, but understanding comes from knowing words. This is why the early stages of education are fundamentally the most important in regards to exposure to vocabulary and expanding their understanding of meaning-rich words – it's environmental.

A LITERAL LITERARY BARRIER

Meaning-rich vocabulary is extremely pupil-specific. We must always remember that 'one child's "huge" is another child's "voracious"'. Here are two case studies of pupils where words were held two very different levels of esteem.

'Huge'

I always remember a specific pupil, and he was representative of 'that type' of pupil. Let's call him Declan. It's easy to look back fondly at that little rascal, but did he make me earn my crust! Wow – it was a slog! A talented footballer, street-wise and popular in school with his peers, but working way below age-related expectations. In the day to day, it was easy to get bogged down, and to a certain extent, there was most likely little more that could have been done for that pupil in Year 5. He was totally turned off to learning, unwilling to even just try. His behaviour was a product of the barriers he encountered in every moment of the day, especially within academia – a literal literary barrier, constructed from living in a word-impoverished environment. Declan misbehaved because he didn't understand enough words (blunt, right?). For this type of pupil, vocabulary and the associated understanding were crucial to be able to function socially, communicate and engage in learning at a fundamental level. Being able to do this would have been a 'huge' success. In the short time Declan was my pupil, by introducing new vocabulary (along with intensive phonics teaching), he began to exert a level of control and enjoyment in knowing and using his new-found vocabulary-based independence.

'Voracious'

The true value of teaching vocabulary discretely came to fruition for me via this pupil and her close peer group. Let's call her Meg. She was an avid reader, a talented writer and extremely hard-working. Her writing was good; she knew all of the checklist features, the grammar, the expanded noun phrases and so on. She could do it all. Teaching vocabulary to Meg was about that next bit – the creation of tension and atmosphere with vocabulary (the bit that's hard to teach). The bit that is easier for children that read, because they're immersed in it all the time. 'Translucent' was the word that had been discretely taught in an earlier lesson, with the knowledge that a dragon would soon be encountered by Sir Lancelot in the text we were reading. We targeted words, such as 'emaciated' too, ready for a piece of writing that was planned for the end of the week. Meg smashed it. Not in the checklist or interim assessment framework sense, but in a sense that mattered to me as I read it. I was proud of her. Her word pool was widening and deepening each day because of her 'voracious' appetite for words, and the impact was clear to for all to see. You can see what she wrote above.

For those two very different pupils, words were valuable in two very contrasting ways. For one pupil, words had the potential to open the door to a world of understanding but that door was stubbornly closed. For the other, words enabled the pupil to walk through the door and become immersed in everything held within. In neither scenario are words any more important or valuable than in the other. In both situations, vocabulary had the power to disable or enable them as learners.

Whether in EYFS, Year 6 or Year 10, the language we choose to teach pupils is of the upmost importance. It's continuous, it builds, it widens and it deepens word by word.

Find opportunities wherever possible to share fabulous examples of word choices.

PRE-TEACHING VOCABULARY FOR READING

The pre-teaching of vocabulary is another pro-active strategy to use within your taught vocabulary arsenal. As alluded to previously, we don't want to hold either taught or encountered vocabulary in any greater esteem than the other. So let's clarify, so as not to confuse. Pre-teaching doesn't mean we are going to laboriously go through a bank of words and explain them all at the beginning of a book. If anything, it's more about a state of preparedness in yourself. You could even say that 'pre' in 'pre-teaching', means being prepared so that you can unleash them at the right moment.

Teach your pupils about words that hold a richness in the context they have been used, but also be aware of words that have the potential to create a barrier to understanding. Think about pupils like Declan and Meg, or even yourself – you don't want to be caught out by a menacingly roguish word, used sublimely by an author, that has you totally foxed. And, although for most teachers this is a very unlikely situation, just think about how much more likely this is to happen to your pupils and what they will feel if it happens too often. By having a greater state of preparedness, we are increasing our learner's capacity to access, understand and engage with the text.

Teacher Glitter
@Teacherglitter

Vocabulary for the first 12 chapters of Rose Muddle to explore sorted @imo0030 @KellieMckelvie @Mr_P_Hillips #readingrocks

9 Aug 2018

The Twitter education community is a fabulous place to gather and magpie ideas for your own teaching practice. Within this community, vocabulary, the role it plays within the classroom and the pedagogy that underpins it is growing in prominence. It's wonderful to see how teachers of all experience levels are honing in on the value that vocabulary can add. The Tweet here is a fabulous example of a state of preparedness shown by a teacher preparing to pre-teach vocabulary within a designated text. Identifying words that are presented in the text and will require additional teaching will require you to pre-read sections of the book ahead of your pupils so that you can be prepared.

The *Vocab in Books* section of the www.verbivoreteacher.com site is a wonderful resource that is in its adolescence but has the potential to be huge for facilitating the pre-teaching and preparation of vocabulary from high-quality texts. *Vocab in Books* is a free, growing library of vocabulary lists for popular books. Each list identifies the vocabulary in a particular passage that might require additional attention or teaching.

The Verbivore website curated by Jack Phillips (@Mr_P_Hillips) has a growing wealth of vocabulary-related resources to use within the classroom. And, importantly, nearly all of it is free. Jack is another passionate teacher who advocates the explicit teaching of vocabulary in schools. As well as the handy *Vocab in Books* section, Verbivore has developed child-friendly characters, 'The Word Gang', to explore morphology, root words, expansive descriptive vocabulary lists and much more. The beauty of resources such as Jack's or ideas such as @TeacherGlitter's, are that you can easily use as little or as much as you require to meet your needs and those of your children – perfect for widening and deepening those pupil word pools!

NINJA REFLECTIONS

Yet again time becomes a factor. 'When am I supposed to fit this all in?' I hear you cry. But, being prepared for the vocabulary that is used within a text will enable you to spend your valuable time in school to far greater effect. I suggest you super-charge your vocabulary book. Make it a hugely valuable resource to work from. Highlight, make notes, underline, annotate key vocabulary in the book you're reading. Once you have done it once, you won't need to do it again and chances are you'll use it time and time again! And remember, not every word will need discussing, but surely it's better to be prepared for the ones that do.

Pre-teach for reading – at a glance

- Pre-read the book you intend to read with the class, teach from or build units of work around.

- Don't be too precious or proud: highlight, makes notes, annotate key vocabulary in the book.

- Use the classroom space and display boards to display vocabulary. (See Chapter 6.)

- Has someone created a resource with identified vocabulary already? If so, use it.

- Only read ahead of the pupils a chapter at a time (everyone can manage this – it's just 10-15 minutes).

- Make the words you find in the book your 'words of the day' – two birds, one stone.

GENERAL UNDERSTANDING OF VOCABULARY

The final rationale for teaching vocabulary for general understanding can be made very simple: there are words that you will inevitably and innocently assume that your pupils know but, believe me, they don't. One of my greatest oversights as a class teacher, and this remains true today, is assuming that a pupil knows what a word means.

Words that you wouldn't especially choose for their depth, their capacity to expand vocabulary or their effect on the atmosphere in a text – I mean '*general*' words that you and many other adults will use in normal everyday activities – they can just wash over your pupils because they don't know what they mean! Here are two very recent examples, both with Year 6 pupils, believe it or not, who both went on to achieve the all-important expected standard in consecutive years.

'Fortnight'

Amidst a conversation linked to half-term, I dared to ask the question, 'Do we all know what a fortnight is?'. I don't even recall why. Uneasy expressions and awkward body language followed. It wasn't just one pupil who didn't know the meaning of the word, although she became the focus of the discussion. It wasn't her fault, she just didn't know what it meant. Now she does, they all do, which is great.

'Countryside'

In a very recent lesson observation, I was keen to impress and had gone all out, only for the lesson to be stopped in its tracks by several pupils who had no idea what 'the countryside' was. Something so very simple that I just assumed all pupils would know. They didn't, but they do now.

The key message here is that every child's vocabulary will vary because of the different environments they experience. We must never assume that a child knows what a word means, we must be vigilant, be ninja and ready to pounce on every opportunity to teach new vocabulary to our pupils and increase their understanding. We can't plan for these words – it's impossible – but because of their 'general' and 'everyday' nature, we can be ready to challenge pupil understanding and ready to seize on every opportunity to increase word wealth.

ENCOUNTERED VOCABULARY

There shouldn't really be a debate about taught (contextless) vs encountered (contextual) vocabulary. Hopefully, you have already begun to understand how they shouldn't be seen as mutually exclusive, but are essential to each other's survival. One can't really be seen to function effectively without the other. If we are to become ninja in the classroom, then every new piece of vocabulary is important, regardless of whether it is taught or encountered.

Encountered vocabulary is quite simply the vocabulary found in a book – the specific, articulate and purposeful word choices that an author makes. It's certainly easy to see why this drum is firmly banged by a whole host of educators and professionals. 'It must be taught in context!' they cry. 'The contexts, atmospheres, emotions, characters and plots give the words a purpose and bring them to life.' This is certainly true. But encountered vocabulary is only valuable to our pupils if *we* have the ninja mentality – that state of preparedness, ready to pounce. Not every teacher in the kingdom is a master of the written word (nor am I). We have to work at it every day, being ready to bring the words to life as we encounter them. The words need to encounter you, you're not to be messed with! You mean business.

Encountered vocabulary, executed with skill, is underpinned by the principals of taught vocabulary – pre-reading and ensuring the vocabulary is ready to encounter you. This mentality is crucial. 'Encountering' something implies that it is an unexpected incident, but we don't really want this to be a recurring pattern. If we encountered wild animals while out walking in the forest each day and didn't modify our behaviour patterns, eventually our luck would run out and we might 'encounter' a bear. Not cool – the consequences would most likely be catastrophic. If we aren't ready to encounter a particular word, then the consequences for our pupils can be just as catastrophic. It may sound a little dramatic, but even the increased contextual value of encountered vocabulary alone won't save you. What you need is an encountered vocabulary mindset.

ENCOUNTERED VOCABULARY MINDSET

Mindset is of paramount importance if you are to become a Vocabulary Ninja. Your thought processes inevitably determine your actions, and your actions will determine any outcomes you hope to achieve. Your mindset is everything. A ninja can be defined as a person who excels in a particular skill. In order to excel and start master vocabulary, you must first master your ninja mindset.

When it comes to encountered vocabulary, we need to be fully prepared. Vocabulary needs to encounter you! Adapting the strategies below will ensure that you make the most of every vocabulary-based encounter that comes your way.

Trim or cut a school book in half or create a folded booklet. Use it as a mini word recorder – The Word Explorer's Journal!

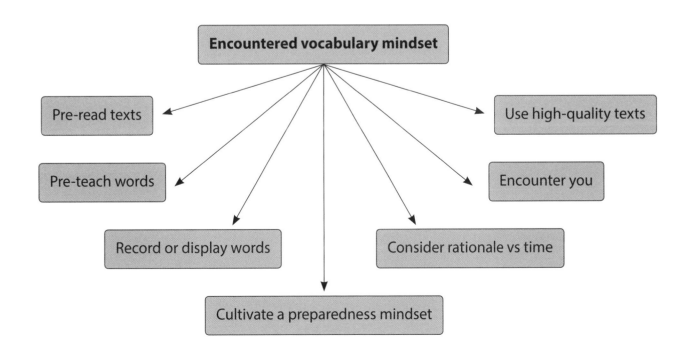

How to 'encounter' vocabulary

Pre-read texts – Pre-read the books that you intend to share with your learners. Highlight, mark and make notes in the text. Be knowledgeable about the literature.

Pre-teach words – Be realistic – you might choose to teach one word from each chapter in greater detail. These words will undoubtedly appear in other texts. These will be uncovered during your pre-read and then planned for.

Record or display words – Any words that you take the time to speak about, knowledge check or teach in greater detail should be recorded somewhere in the classroom for pupils to reference. You could use a working wall, vocabulary books or display. This is crucial if you are to develop independent learners. See Chapter 5.

Cultivate a preparedness mindset – As an adult, you will pre-read a book and make assumptions about the language that is important for your pupils to know; this will also be informed by the words that you know. Be prepared for your best laid plans to be foiled by simple words that your pupils don't understand. Still teach your meaning-rich language, but be prepared for the everyday language barriers that will arise from the text. These words will often need a very brief explanation and then you can simply move on. There isn't time for anything more.

Consider rationale vs time – Not every word can be dissected to a morphological level – let's be real, schools are hectic places to be. A single book will hold thousands of words. What is your rationale for teaching a word? Is it for understanding, for use in writing or to widen vocabulary? Be clear on what you hope to achieve by teaching a word. Think about which words only need a quick understanding check or a ten second explanation and move on. Also think about those meaning-rich words that you want pupils to devour and replicate in their writing – these words might need recording for later.

Encounter you – Just think about being unprepared for an encounter with a wild animal such as a wolf or a bear. The outcome isn't going to be pleasant. It's much better to be ready for those encounters, and it's the same with vocabulary.

Use high-quality texts – Use high-quality texts with your class. Twitter is a wonderful resource to find high-quality texts, from classical authors to ones bursting onto the literary scene!

Remember, there will never be enough time to teach every word. It's impossible. Believe in the value of the words that you have chosen and know that there really is only so much that you can do. Each micro-success and the marginal gains that you make will be of significance in the end.

Huge or voracious, Cornwall or Devon, taught vs encountered – all equally important, equally valuable and equally tasty! There isn't the need to debate which is better, we need them all. By focusing on that very fact, we can begin to think about the explicit instruction of vocabulary and how to make it memorable.

4 – EXPLICIT VOCABULARY INSTRUCTION

This part of the book is where we start to think about explicit vocabulary instruction on a daily basis. Even at this early stage, understanding that explicit vocabulary instruction will make up only a small part of your assault on vocabulary is important; it isn't the only tool you will be using.

If you were to think about our magical target of 50,000 words in a child's working vocabulary, teaching a word a day for seven years would still only equate to 1,330 words for pupils with 100 per cent attendance. This is why explicit vocabulary instruction alone mustn't be your only focus. It must be one of many effective strategies in your vocabulary toolkit which are ready to be used when the opportunity presents itself.

Not every word can be planned for, nor should it be, and so a range of other effective strategies that will be outlined in later chapters should be used in conjunction with explicit vocabulary instruction as part of your teaching repertoire. This is when we begin to think about taught vs encountered vocabulary.

Explicit instruction is still crucial for a number of reasons. As discussed earlier, the role that grammar now plays within the curriculum is significant. Explicit instruction offers a numbers of detailed grammatical avenues to explore with your pupils and, more importantly, the time to do it effectively. Due to the nature of encountered vocabulary, it isn't always planned for, and will only enable a short discussion at that point. Exploring the grammar of encountered vocabulary in detail during a fast-paced English or maths lesson probably wouldn't be good practice.

So, what do we mean by explicit vocabulary instruction? Well, by explicit, I mean 'stated clearly and in detail, leaving no room for confusion or doubt'. This is the single most important principle of teaching vocabulary. Such a fabulous definition, a mantra even! Even in this statement, we are simply discussing teaching and learning.

'Explicit means stated clearly and in detail, leaving no room for confusion or doubt.'

What you do   so that others can learn

(Teaching)   (Learning)

Using the strategies and advice that follow, you can attempt to maximise the effectiveness of the 'what you do' part.

WORD OF THE DAY

Teaching a word of the day (WOD) should be a core component of your vocabulary systems in school. The routine alone – explicitly teaching a single word each day – will benefit your pupils. As stated in previous chapters, your rationale for teaching this word will need to be clear in your mind. Alternatively, *Vocabulary Ninja* provides Grasshopper and Shinobi-level words to teach every day of the academic year. Grasshopper level words are aimed at ages 4-7 and Shinobi level words at 7-11 year old children. The caveat being that we can never pigeonhole a word to a certain age of learner but teach them what they require.

Have the word of the day up when children enter the classroom in the morning. This is purposeful and great for routine.

The principles of teaching a WOD are exactly the same, whether you chose to use a word from *Vocabulary Ninja* or a word of your own. School can be a busy and high-pressure environment, so some days it's good to know that *Vocabulary Ninja* is there – a few clicks and you are ready to go, safe in the knowledge that there will be a high-quality, engaging resource for you to use every day. If you are at the stage of going it alone, *Vocabulary Ninja* provides a range of free resources to teach your own word of the day. See page 6 for more information on how to access free, ready-to-use word of the day resources.

TEN STEPS IN TEN MINUTES (ISH!)

Teaching the word of the day should be a fast-paced, fun and energetic experience for your learners. The following ten steps are crucial to ensuring it is exactly that. Always keep in mind that this short period of time is your domain – you are teaching and the children are learning. This is the 'what you do' period, where you will work to ensure that there is no confusion or doubt for learners.

NINJA NOTES

Ninjas don't like sitting at their desk so get up, move around and create an excitement about the session. Excitement and enthusiasm were never created from sitting at a desk!

Step 1 – Introduce pronunciation (30 seconds)

Introduce the word of the day (WOD) to your learners. (See page 45 for exemplar WODs.) The first step is to orally model the WOD: pronounce it clearly ensuring pupils hear it. Ask the pupils to say the WOD back to you as a group. You may even ask some individuals to repeat it back to you. This may be especially important in regions where certain sound patterns may be affected by dialect or with pupils who you want to ensure are pronouncing the word accurately.

Step 2 – Clap syllables (30 seconds)

This may be incorporated into step 1. Reference the syllables of the word. Model clapping the syllables, and have the children repeat. Don't ask for conjecture from learners about how many syllables a WOD has, just teach it. You could adapt claps into ninja hand chops and kicks, bringing in a kinaesthetic element to the teaching.

Step 3 – Give explicit definition (60 seconds)

We don't want any confusion about the word; be explicit to ensure there is no confusion or doubt about its meaning. Use a child-friendly definition or explain the meaning of the word within the context of the book you are using. Offer additional child-friendly explanation if required. In defining this word, step 4 should naturally follow when discussing the role the WOD plays within the sentence.

Step 4 – Discuss word class (30 seconds)

This is where subject knowledge becomes essential. We don't want to be caught offering cliché definitions of a verb and adjective. The WOD from *Vocabulary Ninja* (page 44) will suggest single or multiple word classes that a target word may be able to function as. For instance, a word may be a noun or a verb depending on the role it plays within a sentence, e.g. 'phone' can be a noun (a phone) or a verb (to phone). Discussing the word class within the exemplar sentence can also be extremely useful.

Step 5 – Display the exemplar sentence (60 seconds)

The exemplar sentence is the first opportunity for learners to see a word in action, allowing for the definition and word class to develop a context in which to be discussed further. Yet again, the exemplar sentence should be as child friendly as possible to aid understanding. Even at this early stage, some learners will have a greater understanding of a word than others, so a child-friendly example that they can use is essential. You may even offer up another sentence orally that can provide further clarity. Try to ensure that all other words in your examples are familiar – we want the only new word to be the WOD.

Step 6 – Oral creation and rehearsal (30 seconds)

Ask learners to orally create their own sentence that includes the WOD and share it with the children next to them or on their table. This will allow pupils to hear ideas and contexts from other pupils, as well as drawing inspiration from the exemplar sentence. Adaptation of the word tense is fine, as some children will naturally develop a sentence in the past tense linked to their own memories. Some children will also, without consciously thinking about it, add prefixes and suffixes to the target word. This can be encouraged and celebrated when sharing; definitely make reference to this and the related grammatical terminology if it happens. The oral creation stage is an important opportunity for you to target specific learners and help develop their ideas. Remember, never assume – earn your pennies, circulate around your learners and impact understanding. In other words, teach.

Step 7 – Orally share (90 seconds)

As we aim to maintain the pace of the session, don't wait for every child to have 'finished' and have a perfect oral sentence to share. Some learners will naturally be ready to share much more quickly. By now, learners will have heard your sentence and three or four examples from the children on their table. Hush the class and ask the children who are ready to start to share their sentence with the class (one at a time). This will ensure that children whose ideas don't come as easily are exposed to further examples of the target word in action and can draw inspiration for themselves. For those children who do have high-quality ideas, refer them to steps 8 and 9 once step 7 is complete.

Step 8 – Orally edit and challenge (60 seconds)

As pupils orally share their sentence with the rest of the class, this is your opportunity to edit the sentences that the pupils have created. This is an extremely powerful tool. We don't want to pick apart every word but selecting a word to improve, correcting the tense or even ensuring subject-verb agreement is in place can be done efficiently at this moment. The great thing about orally editing as you go with pupils is that you can ensure that you are having an instant impact on their understanding. More often than not, the oral feedback you offer to one pupil is pertinent to a group of pupils or even the whole class. Once pupils have shared an idea and you are confident they have grasped the target word, move them quickly on to step 9. Continue to move quickly through the class, listening to and orally editing as many sentences as possible. Steps 7, 8 and 9 could be streamlined further by having any additional adults work specifically with groups of pupils to ensure the process is expedited. Some children won't need any level of oral editing.

Step 9 – Write (180 seconds)

Once orally edited, children should record the sentence they have created. Try to do this in the same place to build a working resource bank of vocabulary for pupils to reference independently. This could be in the back of an English book or a specific vocabulary book.

Step 10 – Share, orally edit and celebrate (60 seconds)

It is crucial to share the written version of the sentence. Pupils will often edit or correct themselves having had the opportunity to read the sentence aloud. If they don't, this is your chance to orally edit the sentence and give some extremely powerful feedback to pupils. Ensure that they immediately act upon that feedback and physically edit their written sentence. At this point, it is also great to remember that one child's 'huge' will be another child's 'voracious'. Celebrate all sentences equally! After you've completed the ten steps, ensure that the WOD is added to your working vocabulary display (see Chapter 5). Having taught the word, you want it to be available for pupils to use and spell independently.

INSTANTANEOUS SUPERFICIAL IMPACT

Most certainly, teaching the word of the day will take a little longer than ten to 15 minutes in the first instance. Your confidence will grow day-by-day and the pupils will become accustomed to the conventions and WOD routine, which will speed up certain aspects of the session. For instance, some pupils will become extremely eager to produce their written sentence as they already have an exciting idea. Don't get in their way – let them go with it and use step 7 and beyond. Undoubtedly, there will be days where the word of the day is easier to process or understand for pupils and other days where words are a little more tricky. An example might be the word 'fastidious', which can't just be shoehorned into a sentence because it requires contextual and conventional understanding from the pupils. In the case of 'fastidious', a little more work will be required to ensure all pupils can access the WOD.

Chill! Don't worry if you have to miss sections out. Sometimes classrooms are busy and things crop up.

One of the subtle brilliances of word of the day is that it has an instantaneous superficial impact and a more meaningful, deeper impact too, much like an asteroid striking the Earth. Smaller asteroids or meteorites strike the Earth every day. They don't change the Earth one by one, but they are noticeable. Over time, small interstellar objects striking the surface of the Earth will change, sculpt and modify its entire complexion, maybe until it is entirely unrecognisable. Word of the day is the same – you will quickly see the WOD cropping up in conversation, and in reading and writing. It's amazing to see! But your daily barrage of discussion, oral editing and challenge, sharing, written opportunities and playfulness with the WOD will have a deeper and more meaningful impact on your pupils. The bonus being that word of the day won't rain down terror and destroy the Earth in a strike!

Be aware that understanding will take time. Yes, we will have that instantaneous superficial impact noticeable in conversation and the pupils' books, which as teachers we all want, but don't get too carried away. Remember that it is the cumulative effect over time – the marginal gains, consistency and quality of your subject knowledge – that will build understanding.

For the ultimate impact, try to embed the word of the day practice in every class across the school. This won't happen overnight, but just imagine the ninja mindset flowing through your school like a river, filling up your pupils' vocabulary puddles and turning them into vast reservoirs! Once it does happen, this is when a cataclysmic change will happen in your school. It will be like the school has actually been hit by a vocabulary asteroid – an extinction-level event and the dawning of a new era. But before all of that can happen, the first meteor has to strike.

5 – THE VOCABULARY ENVIRONMENT – YOUR CLASSROOM

Your classroom has the potential to the biggest and most effective resource in your vocabulary arsenal. Your classroom environment and the routines found within your classroom are crucial in supporting your vocabulary journey and in further developing the independence of your learners. Having effective systems for recording, displaying and referencing vocabulary will enhance all areas of your curriculum and bring writing and oracy to the forefront of your and your learners' attention. Implementing high-quality working walls can prove hugely beneficial. Throwing out the doubled- or triple-backed dormant display rule book and embracing a 'live' display attitude is invaluable. Children will begin to understand that the walls are full of language that has been taught, discussed and previously used; they will understand what it means and be ready to use it.

The only principle that we need to consider while thinking about our environment is that of effectiveness. Ask yourself the question when looking at a display, 'How effective is this display or use of space?' When I say effective, what I really mean is, how does what you have put on the wall help expedite the learning process in your classroom? How does it respond and adapt to your pupils' needs and the progress that they are making day by day? How does it allow them to continue working independently without your support? If it doesn't, then why not?

Does your display look nice? Is it bright and colourful? Is it double-backed? Is it laminated? Does it remain there for a significant period of time? These are all superficial aspects that ultimately add no real determinable value to the learning process. And, they take up a huge amount of someone's time to put up there. I know there will be thousands of very similar displays all around the country (and possibly the world) that are from resource suppliers, and look amazing when you walk into a classroom, but how effective are they really? How often are they referred to in your teaching and learning time? How often do pupils use them independently or refer to them in conversations? I wouldn't hesitate to guess that the answer is 'not often'!

By the way, if this is your classroom right now, this isn't a criticism – no chance. It's a reflection point about how, as ninja practitioners, we can draw upon and improve an aspect of our practice to create yet another marginal gain. Your displays won't revolutionise your outcomes, but what they have the potential to do is enhance your practice by that one per cent. As we have already discussed, one per cent on its own isn't worth writing home about, but the accumulation of marginal gains you have already made are definitely worth significant attention. All of these marginal gains may add up to a ten or 15 per cent change over time. Now who would say no to that?

Correct yourself in front of pupils and staff. Model the thinking behind your word choices.

LIVE, RESPONSIVE AND IMMERSIVE ENVIRONMENT

Let's begin to think about effective strategies for recording, displaying and referencing vocabulary in your classroom as aspects that are worth investing your time in. By developing simple routines and investing a small amount of preparation time into your resources, you will quickly super-charge your classroom environment and make it a live, responsive and immersive environment where pupil independence is high and outcomes across the curriculum are improved.

The vocabulary display strategies model I will explain here shows the journey that a piece of vocabulary takes from source through to independent use by pupils and learners within the enabled environment. The model demonstrates how a vocabulary-enabled environment can contribute to increased independence over time and thus improve outcomes.

VOCABULARY DISPLAY STRATEGIES MODEL (2018)

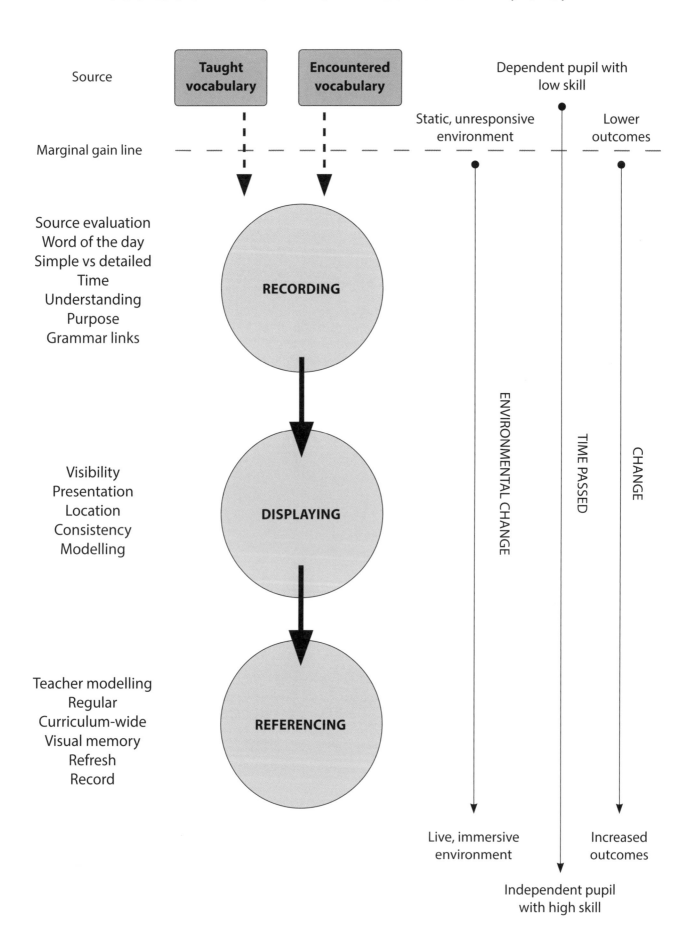

Vocabulary Ninja © Andrew Jennings, 2019

The source

Before we start to think about how we will record vocabulary, it is crucial to think about the source of our vocabulary. The source of vocabulary will directly affect how we respond and what actions we take. Vocabulary will either be taught, e.g. word of the day, or it will be encountered incidentally, e.g. in books, conversations and other stimuli that we hadn't necessarily planned on teaching. Even though we had not planned on teaching this language, as a Vocabulary Ninja, we need to be ready to pounce on these opportunities when they arise.

The marginal gain line

One of the most interesting factors within the model is the 'marginal gain line', which links to overall classroom display effectiveness. Thinking again about the world of sport, the gain line is the line showing the positive progress you have made on the playing field with respect to where you first started. We can take this principle and adapt it to vocabulary display within the classroom and the marginal gains we hope to make by adapting our display practice. The model suggests that unless vocabulary reaches the recording, displaying and referencing stages, we cannot make positive progress beyond the marginal gain line. In essence, a huge of amount of vocabulary is lost because in the first instance it isn't recorded and/or displayed. In the end, it becomes nearly impossible to effectively refer back to it or for all pupils to use it with independence and skill. Just imagine how much vocabulary is lost or how many times our pupils miss the opportunity to embed a word into their working vocabulary. In order for pupils to start making the improvements we so desire, vocabulary has to cross the 'marginal gain line' and progress through the subsequent stages.

These are the three clear stages in the vocabulary display strategies model: recording, displaying and referencing vocabulary. These three stages all occur *after* vocabulary has been taught or encountered. Within the three core stages of effective vocabulary display strategies, there are also sub-categories that should be considered at each stage. Some of these considerations can be built into an efficient recording, displaying and referencing routine within the classroom.

Preparation

Like any journey, we must be prepared and well-resourced if we are to reach the promised land. Most school supply cupboards and teacher stationery drawers will contain all of the basic supplies that you will require.

Vocabulary display essentials:

- A4 and A3 card of various colours, trimmed into different lengths, shapes and sizes
- Marker pens of various colours
- Meter stick (or large ruler)
- Sticky tack
- Drawing pins
- Pegs
- String
- Flip chart paper

Ensure all adults in your classroom understand the new resources and routines. This can help increase their effectiveness and impact.

Have all of these resources readily available, pre-cut and waiting to be accessed at a moment's notice. This will enable you to build the immersive and responsive, word-rich classroom that you are aiming for. The added bonus is that your pupils will love it even more if they are involved in the process of building and adding to it. Nothing here is a huge revelation – anyone can implement this simple and effective preparation in 15-20 minutes and then be well stocked up for a unit of work and beyond.

Having these resources hanging in folders or units from the display will make it simpler to add vocabulary as it arises.

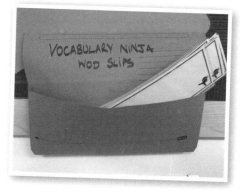

A little bravery is required here. That pristine, laminated display is great, and I'm sure that the 25-30 hours' work that went into creating it was worthwhile but now I want you to tear it down, leaving only a blank display board with possibly some awesome lettering. With this, you're ready to go. The vocabulary and phrases will be added *slowly*, but they will create a meaningful display over time, one that has a clear purpose and a role within your classroom. Your teaching assistant or meaningful others will also thank you for not asking them to spend a huge amount of time and money on printing and laminating generic display paraphernalia (what a word by the way!).

Once you have your essentials assembled, or once you have assembled your essentials (whichever you prefer), you are ready to begin your display adventure and give your classroom a literary heartbeat.

Recording

How you record your vocabulary will depend on the source – whether it is taught or encountered. Has it come from the word of the day, from your class novel, a conversation or your literacy lesson? This is important to be ready for.

As mentioned in Chapter 4, your word of the day instruction is a closed procedure with a very clearly defined process and outcomes. As suggested, it is good practice for pupils to have the opportunity to write experimental sentences as part of the word of the day activity. This might be in the back of their literacy books or even in another 'vocabulary book' that you use (teachers usually get rather creative with such things). This is all fabulous to see. However, we must consider how readily available the WODs are, that we have spent so much valuable time teaching. I would advise that your classroom has some direct way of *recording* and *displaying* your WODs, so that they can be *referenced* independently by your pupils at any time of the day (notice the record, display and reference cycle).

Use the windows! Grab some fluorescent drywipe pens and record WODs on the windows. #marginalgains

Ensuring that words are recorded and displayed effectively means that pupils can, and will, use them independently across the school day and hopefully beyond. It also means that any word can be referenced at any point of the day. You'll be surprised at the number of opportunities you will find to refer back to the WODs you have displayed. A very simple, yet effective, process.

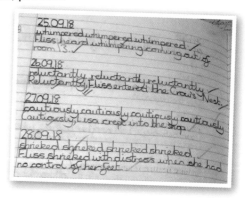

Here is a further example of how the WOD might be progressively recorded in the back of a literacy book. The example shows the learner actively experimenting with the WOD. If the vocabulary book is available in lessons, it serves as a useful reference point for pupils during lessons.

Deciding whether to record a word in a simple or more detailed manner will depend on a range of factors. Time, desired outcome, children's current level of understanding, value, usefulness, possible modifications, and links to spelling, punctuation, grammar and purpose will all affect whether or not you choose to record a word in a simple or detailed fashion. It is prudent to ensure that any detailed recording of vocabulary, which will undoubtedly take up more time, has a clear purpose. These will most likely be words that you purposefully choose to introduce to pupils via the word of the day activity, from a class text and so on. In terms of outcomes, the words you choose to record and display in a more detailed fashion may have been chosen with the knowledge that the words will become essential language for an upcoming piece of writing or drama that the pupils are creating.

You could record the WOD simply (using the working wall explained above), or you could record it in detail. The source is irrelevant really; the key thing here is to ensure that if you and the children are going to spend time recording it in a detailed manner, the outcomes are worth it. In contrast, sometimes it will simply be highly effective to come across a word, celebrate and explain it, record it (two to three minutes, if that) and move on. Boom – done – slap it up on the word wall! The word has been efficiently recorded, effectively displayed, and now it's available to be referenced readily.

If and when you record a word to be displayed, please write it large enough and clearly enough for every pupil in the room to be able to see it. Too many times, words are recorded (which is amazing), then displayed, but the words are so small that children are required to move much closer, squint even, to see the language. When it comes to recording vocabulary, bigger is better.

NINJA NOTES

If your writing isn't clear, get a pupil or another adult in the classroom to do it.

Displaying

Now you've recorded your vocabulary, in a legible style and in an appropriate font size, you're ready to display your vocabulary.

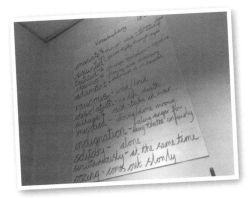

A Vocabulary Ninja classroom where vocabulary is added as part of all aspects of the curriculum.

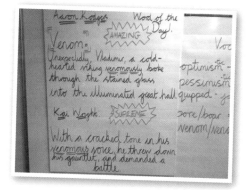

An example vocabulary display with consistent colours, formats and reference points. Pupils enjoy experimenting with vocabulary and being part of the recording and display process.

Content that has been taught over a period of several months should be displayed around the classroom on flipchart paper in the form of a poster. Once this information has been on display and referred to regularly, ask pupils to close their eyes and prompt them to point to the posters that you specify. By displaying important taught content around the classroom, and referring to it regularly, you can help create a picture in pupils' heads of where this familiar information prompt is held. One important factor to note is that when the displayed content is referred to, you should adjust your location in the classroom and stand next to the content you are referring to.

Pupils will develop excellent visual retention of the locations of the content. They will be able to discuss what information was in that location and refer to the details. All of the vocabulary and content that you display must be placed intentionally so that it is visible from any seating position in the classroom. Washing lines and pegs can be used to hang language in prominent positions within the classroom. The use of colour is important to stimulate memory and aid recall within the pupils' brains; try to develop a consistent system or pattern when choosing which colour to use. One other area to consider when displaying vocabulary is your modelling and presentation. As a Vocabulary Ninja, you have high standards, you are methodical and are the exemplar that all grasshoppers look towards for guidance.

Before you display anything you have recorded, be sure to think about the location of the vocabulary you wish to present. How visible is it to everyone? Is it large enough to see and is it written clearly enough for all pupils to use independently, without guidance? Does this mean that words need to be printed rather than joined, so that there are no grey areas? Clarity is key. Once you have begun to display vocabulary, how consistently are you recording and displaying the language? Can you create coloured patterns that will aid how effectively your pupils will reference and retain the language? For instance, when you write a verb, can it always be green (or another designated colour)? When you write an adjective, can it always be red? This consistency of colour will aid your pupils' retention. You wouldn't need to do it for every word class – nouns, verbs, adjectives and conjunctions would be fine to begin with.

That's right – there's lots to think about! And you thought displays were straightforward! Well, they are – yours are now going to be just a little bit more ninja.

Referencing

So, you have recorded lots of awesome vocabulary that you have taught and encountered, you have displayed it effectively so that everyone can see it – you are nearly there and should be commended for your efforts so far. The final stage is referencing the vocabulary that you have recorded and displayed.

Referencing is all about your practice, embedding high-quality language into all aspects of your life within the classroom. Why? Well, if you model it, then the children will begin to replicate your ninja attitude towards words. Emphasise the fact that you are referring back to where the language has been displayed when you use it. Point, gesticulate and orally model your intentions close to the language. The Grand Masters amongst us will have pre-taught language that will occur in future chapters of class texts or literature you are using, thus creating the awe-inspiring moment when the word we recently taught miraculously turns up in the literature. Perfect!

Find opportunities to use the words that have been displayed in your day to day language. If 'tedious' is now on the wall, reference the wall and use the word. Model, explain why you made this language choice, and ask the children why they think you made this choice. What is the effect of using it? This will help knowledge retention and deepen pupils' understanding of the word. If this becomes a staple practice of your classroom, then your pupils will eventually begin to replicate your vocabulary choices and practices.

Squeeze referenced words into assemblies and model making enhanced vocabulary choices when you make a poor one. #powerfulstuff

It was once said that people will only use the vocabulary that their environment demands of them. So the message is clear: I demand that you create an environment that demands more of your pupils. It is your responsibility to create a living, breathing, word-rich environment that demands everything from your grasshoppers, and yourself. You all deserve it. I know that much is true.

Sometimes space is limited. If you can't have an immersive classroom where vocabulary is dominant on all four walls, at least create a dedicated space for it to be accessible.

PART 2 ⚊

VOCABULARY NINJA TEACHING TOOLKIT

Any ninja needs his or her tools. In this case, our tools are our vocabulary teaching resources. We have already began to adopt a ninja mindset and evaluated our classroom effectiveness. We now need to arm ourselves with tried-and-tested resources that are guaranteed to bring vocabulary to life in the classroom.

So let's dive straight in and explore the resources!

Each of the resources that you uncover within this chapter will be available online. See page 6 for more information about how to access these resources.

WORD OF THE DAY

This chapter is where your word of the day journey truly begins. It contains sample Grasshopper level words and sample Shinobi level words ready to use in the classroom. More resources are also available in the online resources for this book (see page 6 for more information).

Grasshopper and Shinobi words aren't about a level or status. As alluded to before, one child's 'huge' is another child's 'voracious'. Grasshopper words are simpler words that children are more likely to have heard before and in most instances will be simpler to apply. Thus, Grasshopper words tend to be used with children who have developing word pools, most likely our younger learners. I think it is important not to put an age on a word as it gives the message that it is only appropriate for some people to use it, and this is fundamentally wrong. Grasshopper words will often have a range of closely linked synonyms that make it much easier to understand and use. Shinobi words, on the other hand, may have a greater level of complexity that requires life experiences and grammatical understanding to not only comprehend them, but use them incisively. Shinobi words often have very few or no synonyms, and they have a very distinct purpose, meaning they can't just 'replace' a word as a Grasshopper word might be able to.

Each word of the day (WOD) comes complete with a comprehensive breakdown of the word. First and foremost, the WOD is split into syllables. Referencing the syllable count is often a great strategy to support spelling for pupils, so referring to this daily is extremely effective.

Each WOD is identified within a word class. Some may have two or three word classes that can be applied. For instance, a word may possibly be used as a noun, verb or adjective depending on its role within a sentence. It is crucial to discuss the word class with pupils, making clear the role the word plays within the sentence. The example sentence will only model the word in one context (as a verb, for instance), so it will certainly be good practice to be armed with

another example that uses the word within a different word class – or at least be knowledgeable enough to discuss it further. This is why (as mentioned earlier in the book) subject knowledge is crucial when teaching vocabulary; it can be quite easy to become unstuck.

The definition comes next. The child-friendly definitions can make explaining the meaning of a word much easier. Often, when trying to define a word, children will use the target word over and over rather than explaining the meaning of the word. I would often say to pupils, 'Imagine the person you are talking to has never heard this word before. Simply saying the word you are trying to explain again and again, won't help them understand.'

The definition is followed by the exemplar sentence with the target word in bold. The example sentences are often based around the school day or experiences that a child is likely to be familiar with, especially at Grasshopper level. Where possible, Shinobi-level words are pitched within a familiar context, but this isn't always the case. It's also important to note that the target word isn't always used in the same tense as it is presented at the top of the page. Words will often be used in varied tenses, which of course offers another important discussion point.

Pupils must understand that words can be manipulated and modified to suit the sentence they are creating. This leads nicely into the modifications identified at the bottom of the page. Synonyms and antonyms are great to discuss as they can often increase understanding through association to words that learners already understand. Prefix and suffix understanding is crucial to allow pupils to apply words in various tenses, with different meaning and correct spelling. Referring daily to spelling conventions linked to prefixes and suffixes is guaranteed to improve the accuracy of independent spelling.

All in all, the Word of the day is a comprehensive resource designed to simplify and supercharge a small part of each teaching day.

WORD OF THE DAY
cover

Word class:	noun or verb	Pronunciation:	cov-er

Definition:	If you **cover** something, you place something over it so that it can't be seen.

Example:	It's important to **cover** your mouth when you cough.

Synonym:	Antonym:	Prefix:	Suffix:
protect, shield	reveal	un-, re-, under-	-ed, -ing, -er

Use the word of the day in a compound sentence.

WORD OF THE DAY
thought

Word class:	noun	Pronunciation:	thought

Definition:	A **thought** is an idea from your mind.

Example:	Christopher has a **thought**, so he whispered it to Paola.

Synonym:	Antonym:	Prefix:	Suffix:
idea, notion		after-, fore-	-ful, -less

Use the word of the day in a single clause sentence.

WORD OF THE DAY
balance

Word class:	noun or verb	Pronunciation:	bal-ance

Definition:	If you **balance** something, you place it so that it does not fall one way or the other. The weight is spread equally.

Example:	Emily **balanced** the apple on top of her head.

Synonym:	Antonym:	Prefix:	Suffix:
	instability	im-, over-, un-	-ed, -ing, -er

Use the word of the day in a compound sentence.

WORD OF THE DAY
adopt

Word class:	verb	Pronunciation:	a-dopt

Definition:	If you **adopt** something, you make it your own. This could be a child, a mindset or a point of view.

Example:	The children had begun to **adopt** a more positive attitude towards their work.

Synonym:	Antonym:	Prefix:	Suffix:
embrace acquire	abandon	re-	-ed, -ing, -tion

Use the word of the day in a single clause sentence.

Vocabulary Ninja © Andrew Jennings, 2019

WORD OF THE DAY
establish

Word class:	verb	Pronunciation:	es-tab-lish

Definition:	If you **establish** something you agree that it is true or have proof that shows that it is true.

Example:	The evidence **established** his date of birth, which was previously unknown.

Synonym:	Antonym:	Prefix:	Suffix:
begin initiate	demolish	dis- ,re-	-ed, -ment, -ing

Use the word of the day in a compound sentence.

WORD OF THE DAY

perish

Word class:	verb	Pronunciation:	per-ish

Definition:	If something **perishes** it is no longer alive or it no longer exits.

Example:	The vegetables **perished** during the drought.

Synonym:	Antonym:	Prefix:	Suffix:
expire spoil	survive		-ed, -ing, -able

Use the word of the day in a question.

WORD OF THE DAY
measure

Word class:	noun or verb	Pronunciation:	meas-ure

Definition:	If you **measure** something, you might identify how long, heavy or loud it is using a standard measure.

Example:	Paul's happiness could be **measured** by the number of coffees he drank that day.

Synonym:	Antonym:	Prefix:	Suffix:
weigh evaluate	estimate guess	counter-, re-, im-	-ed, -s, -ing

 Use the word of the day in a compound sentence.

WORD OF THE DAY
dwindle

Word class:	verb	Pronunciation:	dwin-dle

Definition:	If something **dwindles**, it reduces in size or number.

Example:	Roger's energy showed no signs of **dwindling**.

Synonym:	Antonym:	Prefix:	Suffix:
diminish reduce, decrease	increase		-ed, -ing

NINJA CHALLENGE Use the word of the day in a multi-clause sentence.

 Vocabulary Ninja © Andrew Jennings, 2019

VOCABULARY LABORATORY

The Vocabulary laboratory allows pupils to explore a word via a range of tasks and challenges. It is very straightforward to use.

Vocabulary Ninja has developed a passion for the science of words after spending a great deal of time with my close friend, Dr Henrich Frankenstein. Just as Dr Frankenstein studied chemical processes and the decay of living beings to gain an insight into the creation of life, so Vocabulary Ninja is fascinated with the anatomical breakdown of words and insights into the creation of language and life! *Evil laugh ensues*

The Vocabulary laboratory is a versatile resource designed to allow pupils to dive deep into the inner workings of a single word. One of the most impressive aspects of the Vocabulary laboratory is the incidental spelling, punctuation and grammar learning that can be gleaned from the accurate dissection of a word.

An interesting thing about the Vocabulary laboratory is that you will begin to get an amazing perspective into your pupils' lives – a great way to get to know them and personalise learning! Why? Well, because in the first instance, your pupils will apply the word to their own personal experiences. This reinforces my earlier comments about a pupils' limited vocabulary pools being directly linked to their experiences of life. When you first start to use the Vocabulary laboratory resource and children have to apply the new word in their own context, I can near guarantee you will hear a significant number of sentences linked to

'my dog', 'my mum', 'my dad', 'my nana' and so on. It actually becomes amusing how many words can be accurately and humorously applied to 'my dad', 'my dog', 'my mum', 'my house' and so on. These are all people and places that your children are very familiar with, especially your less frequent readers. This is because some pupils will have very few 'varied and rich' experiences from their home-life to apply the new language to. In this context, whole-class texts are a great way of providing a shared experience within your classroom, which all children can use and apply a word to.

The Vocabulary laboratory is a simple yet highly effective resource that can be used with learners of all ages. The following pages provide an annotated Vocabulary laboratory for reference, a complex blank version of the resource for photocopying and a simpler version for younger learners.

ESSENTIAL KNOWLEDGE

On the next page you will find the annotated example of the Vocabulary laboratory with the essential terminology you will need. Along with the basics, you should also make sure you are secure in your understanding of morphology – how words are put together.

Target word – Add the word that you want to focus on. This could be taken from the word of the day, a book or a conversation.

Word class – Word class can offer up some scintillating discussions, especially when the modifications to the word change the word class. By discussing all the subtleties and demonstrating them, we can create stronger links to the rest of the curriculum.

Define it – This is where you can embed the use of dictionary skills and locate an accurate definition of the target word. These skills are essential.

Synonyms and antonyms – Synonyms are words that have the same meaning as the target word. The Vocabulary laboratory gives pupils the chance to discuss and record words that have the same meaning. Antonyms are words that have the opposite meaning and can also be recorded in the Vocabulary laboratory. Often, a pupil's limited vocabulary can have a far-reaching impact on their communication skills and writing outcomes in education. Having regular opportunities to discuss synonyms and antonyms is important.

Break it down – Morphology is the study of the structure of words, essentially what the Vocabulary laboratory is all about. In this section, we want pupils to think about the target word on a morphological level – how the word is made up. Quite often, this will link nicely to the syllables a word contains but not always. Being aware of a word's syllable count is also a fantastic strategy for spelling. The word 'convention', for example, can be broken down into a prefix, root and suffix (con-vent-ion) and it has three syllables. This section of the Vocabulary laboratory may need more time being taught and discussed with the whole class to ensure understanding.

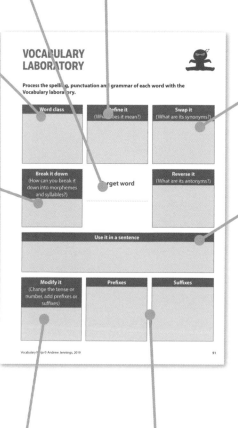

Use in a sentence – It is crucial that pupils have the opportunity to experiment and apply their understanding of a target word. This section provides a safe space for pupils to create sentences, edit and refine their ideas. This is also a fabulous opportunity to challenge pupils. Can they use a certain writing feature, such as a relative clause, thus embedding a range of other writing conventions? Drawing a picture adds to the aesthetic value of the learning, but also acts as a powerful tool for memorisation.

Modify it – Modifications are generally where the root of the word remains constant with various prefixes and suffixes being added to modify the word and its meaning. Depending on the target word you choose, a variety of different prefixes and suffixes will be available for pupils to modify the word meaning and the associated word class. The spelling, punctuation and grammar links here are endless. Spelling rules and strategies, tenses, plurals and rhymes can go here too.

Prefixes and suffixes – An understanding of how prefixes are attached to the beginning of words and suffixes to the end, and how they modify the meaning of the word, are essential skills for pupils to master. Regular use of the Vocabulary laboratory resource will expose pupils to a broad range of prefixes.

VOCABULARY LABORATORY

Process the spelling, punctuation and grammar of each word with the Vocabulary laboratory.

Word class	**Define it** (What does it mean?)	**Swap it** (What are its synonyms?)

Break it down (How can you break it down into morphemes and syllables?)	**Target word**	**Reverse it** (What are its antonyms?)

Use it in a sentence

Modify it (Change the tense or number, add prefixes or suffixes)	**Prefixes**	**Suffixes**

VOCABULARY LABORATORY

Process the spelling, punctuation and grammar of each word with the Vocabulary laboratory.

Target word

_____

Define it

Use it in a sentence

Draw it

CONJUNCTION MALFUNCTION

The Conjunction malfunction resource is designed to explore pupils' understanding of coordinating and subordinating conjunctions. Children simply have to decide which conjunction to place in the space provided. You may need to focus on ensuring that children understand a variety of different conjunctions and can recall them reliably.

ESSENTIAL KNOWLEDGE

Coordinating conjunctions

for, and, nor, but, or, yet, so

Coordinating conjunctions are used to join two independent clauses. Usually an independent clause will contain a subject and a verb, while the coordinating conjunction defines the relationship between the two clauses.

Subordinating conjunctions

although, when, because, meanwhile, however (not exhaustive)

Subordinating conjunctions normally introduce a subordinate clause. The subordinate clause needs to be used in conjunction with an independent clause in order to act as a coherent sentence.

Each conjunction should be taught as part of your English lessons, making explicit reference to the role of each individual conjunction. The different roles are important – by only referring to them as coordinating or subordinating conjunctions, you imply that they have the same role, but this is not the case.

DIFFERENTIATION

Older or more confident pupils might be pushed to focus on the use of subordinating conjunctions, whereas younger or less confident pupils might continue to focus on coordinating conjunctions.

REUSE AND REFINE

One way to take Conjunction malfunction to the next level is to track conjunction use within the class text that you are reading. Make a record of the sentences and the conjunctions used, blank them out and use the text in exactly the same way as the worksheets on the next pages.

Have pupils create a bank of their own sentences and ask them to blank out the conjunction, then share with a partner.

Embed conjunctions in your topic work. Create a bank of sentences with missing conjunctions that are all associated with Vikings or friction, or whichever topic your class are studying.

NINJA NOTES

For younger or less confident pupils, a simple conjunction word bank can be useful. When writing, they can refer back to it and see what their options are. #challengeforall #noninjaleftbehind

CONJUNCTION MALFUNCTION

Add the correct subordinating conjunction to the table below.

Clause 1	Subordinating conjunction	Clause 2
I felt ill during the journey		had a short nap and a drink of water.
Fred is tall and blonde,		his brother has long dark hair.
You won't succeed		you work hard.
I love Elliot's work		he uses colour so precisely.
We played charades all evening		we had nothing else to do.
Claire has ridden horses		she was five years old.
She always feeds the cat		she goes to school.
I will be terribly sad		you leave me all alone in the house.
Lucy decided to go outside		it was raining heavily.
Mary closed the shop		she drank some water.
The dog wanted to go for a walk		his owner wasn't so keen.
The class of children were happy		Mrs. Jones visited the school.
We couldn't go to the waterpark		it was closed today.
Don't go back into the building		it is safe to do so.
Danny tied his laces carefully		he ran onto the football pitch.
John had been listening carefully		Phillip hadn't paid any attention.

CONJUNCTION MALFUNCTION

Add the correct coordinating conjunction to the table below.

Clause 1	Coordinating conjunction	Clause 2
I am going shopping,		I am getting my hair cut.
Jerry wanted to make an apple pie		there were no apples left on the tree.
It was raining,		they went to the restaurant.
Oliver was a great striker,		he loved playing in goal.
Sam did not brush his hair,		did he clean his teeth.
Claire hated peas,		she still ate a spoonful.
Paul filled the bucket with water,		Mary dug a huge hole in the sand.
Fran studied a lot,		she didn't pass the test.
You can buy a new phone,		you can borrow my old one.
Daniel was hungry,		he ate a snack.
Jack was unkind to his friends,		he didn't mean to be.
I need to find a new job,		I am unemployed.
My dad doesn't like to cook,		he does it anyway.
He could go to school,		he could stay at home.
I have got a bicycle,		I haven't got a scooter.
You can make your own costume,		just hire one from the shop.

WHICH SENTENCE?

Which sentence? is a multiple-choice resource where children need to decide which sentence is punctuated correctly. Children will be presented with a variety of sentence types that contain grammatical errors. Only one sentence is correct, but which sentence is it?

ESSENTIAL KNOWLEDGE

A working understanding of the four main sentence types can help support pupils' understanding and success in identifying which sentence is correct. The four main sentence types are: exclamations, questions, commands and statements.

Pupils will also need a working understanding of how we use capital letters in sentence structure and for proper nouns. The sentences will challenge their understanding of question marks, exclamation points, commas for clarity, commas in lists and even the punctuation found in speech.

NINJA NOTES

Encourage pupils to spot the basics that are missing from a sentence. Capital letters at the beginning, no full stop, names without capital letters. These sentences can be discounted instantly without much effort, meaning rather than having four to decide from, they might only have two.

WHICH SENTENCE?

Which sentence uses **capital letters** correctly?	Tick one.
thomas, alex and mark visited London on Monday	
Thomas, Alex and Mark visited London on Monday.	
Thomas, Alex and Mark visited London on monday.	
Thomas, alex and Mark visited london on Monday.	

Which sentence is **punctuated** correctly?	Tick one.
Behind the door which was oak stood the phantom.	
Behind the door, which was oak, stood the phantom.	
Behind the door which was oak, stood the phantom.	
Behind the door, which was oak stood the phantom.	

Which sentence is **punctuated** correctly?	Tick one.
The little girl "squealed, I'm hungry and need feeding."	
The little girl squealed, "I'm hungry and need feeding."	
The little girl squealed, "I'm hungry" and need feeding.	
The little girl squealed, "Im hungry and need feeding."	

Which sentence uses **clean** as an **adjective**?	Tick one.
You should clean your teeth.	
Please clean your room before I arrive home.	
We need to clean the car today.	
His face was now extremely clean.	

Which sentence needs an **exclamation mark**?	Tick one.
The sky was bright blue	
She said the sun was so lovely	
What an amazing party that was	
The parks were extremely pretty	

WHICH SENTENCE?

Which sentence uses **coach** as a **verb**?	Tick one.
The coach rolled into the car park.	
The team were waiting for their coach to arrive to training.	
I will coach the junior team today.	
I would prefer to travel on the coach, rather than the train.	

Which sentence is the most **formal**?	Tick one.
You can come to my party if you wish.	
Please come to my party.	
Would you like to attend my party?	
I would be delighted if you could attend my birthday party.	

Which sentence contains an **embedded clause**?	Tick one.
The girl, who I met at the cinema, is in my class at school.	
The team is going to play on Saturday.	
Tom said he wanted to learn to ride a bike.	
Whenever they have time, they like to sit and read.	

Which sentence contains three **prepositions**?	Tick one.
Look around the corner and see who is coming.	
Tom is next to Fred, who is sat on the table near the door.	
Ellie has been waiting to visit the fair all week.	
Down by the river you can find all sorts of cool stones.	

Which sentence uses **park** as a **verb**?	Tick one.
Dad needed to park the car close to the entrance.	
Can we visit the park today?	
John scored his best time at the Park Run.	
They couldn't wait to get inside the waterpark.	

    Vocabulary Ninja © Andrew Jennings, 2019

NOUN VS VERB

This is a classic Vocabulary Ninja resource, and one that I am very proud of. Noun vs verb drills down into pupils' understanding of word class in context. Depending on the sentence, a word could be taking on the role of a noun or a verb. Pupils will need to decide which side they are on when it comes to Noun vs verb.

ESSENTIAL KNOWLEDGE

Nouns

Pupils must understand what a noun is and the role it plays within a sentence. A noun is a word class that names something. Nouns name places, people, objects, emotions, thoughts and so on. They can also broken down into subcategories, e.g. proper nouns, common nouns and abstract nouns.

Verbs

Verbs are often known as 'doing words'. This phrase unfortunately doesn't help pupils fully grasp what a verb is and the role it has in a sentence. Verbs show the states of being, doing and having; *be*, *do* and *have* are all verbs. Being able to identify the subject or object within a sentence can also help identify the verb.

Understanding words within the sentence context

Pupils must understand that certain words, for example the word *walk*, can act as a noun or a verb, depending on the sentence. For instance, if you were to 'go for a walk', *walk* in this context would be a noun. Whereas, if you were to 'walk along the street', *walk* would be a verb. Sometimes the word or phrase that precedes the target word (in this instance 'walk'), can help us decide whether it is a noun or verb. If the word is preceded by an article or determiner, e.g. *a* walk or *the* walk, this helps us know that the target word is a noun. A verb will often be preceded by the word *to*, an auxiliary verb or even a pronoun, e.g. 'I walk', 'we walk'.

NINJA NOTES

Images or small video clips, or drama exercises, are great for illustrating the difference between a noun and a verb to pupils. Give them the same word in two different sentences and ask them to act it out. How does the target word function?

NOUN VS VERB

Decide if the target word is being used as a noun or a verb.

Target word	Context	Word class
crush	There was a crush in the corridor before playtime.	
bottle	We needed to bottle as much water as possible.	
paint	Everyone used the paint with care and attention.	
watch	His watch had stopped working.	
block	He raised his hand to block the sunlight.	
arm	They need to arm themselves before the battle begins.	
picture	He couldn't picture everybody playing nicely together.	
level	Jimmy used the spade to level off the ground.	
clap	Mr. Rogers could hear a clap, but wasn't sure where.	
peel	Next to the bin, there was lots of fruit peel on the floor.	
spoon	Helen was asked to spoon the sand into the tray.	
fire	There was a huge fire which could be seen for miles.	
light	As it was bedtime, Alex needed to switch off his light.	
dip	Peter wanted to dip his biscuit into the warm tea.	
cover	The book cover was tatty and frayed at the edges.	
book	Mum needed to book the tickets before they left.	
train	We need to train harder if we are to win the competition.	
frown	My frown just couldn't be turned upside down.	

Vocabulary Ninja © Andrew Jennings, 2019

SPaG FACTS AND SPaG SPOTTER

The SPaG facts exercise outlines some of the basic terminology that we want all pupils to be able to identify and understand.

SPaG facts are the building blocks of spelling, punctuation and grammar. Pupils will need to be able to carry out simple tasks that require them to understand some of the most basic aspects of SPaG such as identifying word classes, using the correct determiners, adding punctuation and much more. SPaG spotter explores a whole host of spelling, punctuation and grammar issues. 'So what do the pupils have to do?' I hear you ask. They have to spot the SPaG! Simple, but super effective. Children will need to spot the indicated SPaG elements within each sentence. It's great practice and great fun.

ESSENTIAL KNOWLEDGE

SPaG facts and SPaG spotter are comprehensive tools for investigating word classes and grammar in sentences.

Pronouns

I, he she, we, they, those, her, his

Pronouns can replace nouns, help to build cohesion and avoid repetition.

Determiners

a, an, the, this, that, those, these, a few, many, numbers and pronouns

Determiners do what they say: they help us determine noun groups, tense, quantity and possession.

Articles

a, an, the

Articles are used to refer to nouns; there are three of them in English.

Modal verbs

will, might, could, won't, can't, may, can, must

Modal verbs help suggest degrees of possibility, from impossible to certainty.

Nouns

Refer to the Noun vs verb resource (page 59) for more information.

Adjectives

Commonly known as 'describing words' in the classroom, but calling adjectives describing words doesn't help pupils fully understand their purpose. Adjectives have a close relationship with nouns – they help add information and detail about the noun. Adjectives often come before nouns.

Verbs

Refer to the Noun vs verb (page 59) resource for more information.

Adverbs

Adverbs can offer increasing levels of detail to a verb by 'adding' information to the 'verb', thus the term 'adverb'.

Prepositions

on, in, over, under, next to, below, before, after, inside, through

Prepositions tell us more information about an object's location in place or time. A great way of remembering what a preposition tells us about is to spot the word 'position' in 'preposition'.

Conjunctions

Refer to the Conjunction malfunction resource (page 53) for more information.

Don't use SPaG cliché phrases. Be incisive with your feedback and give examples of SPaG in context.

SPaG FACTS

Give examples of these types of word.

noun		possessive pronoun	
verb		subordinating conjunction	
adjective		coordinating conjunction	
adverb		proper noun	
pronoun		collective noun	
article		abstract noun	
determiner		concrete noun	
preposition		quantifier	

Rewrite these words in their expanded form.

can't	
isn't	
won't	
couldn't	
mustn't	
didn't	
I'll	

Rewrite these words in the past tense.

kick	
move	
catch	
remain	
fight	
perform	
blow	

Circle apostrophes for possession.

Jenny's car	We mustn't
I'll be late	Mark's dinner
The man's hat	Don't

Circle the modal verbs.

would	might
fill	park
should	may

SPaG FACTS

Give examples of these types of word.

noun		possessive pronoun	
verb		subordinating conjunction	
adjective		coordinating conjunction	
adverb		proper noun	
pronoun		collective noun	
article		abstract noun	
determiner		concrete noun	
preposition		quantifier	

Add punctuation accurately.

,	Under the table the slimy frog jumped onto my foot.
.	I love ice cream
?	Who is it
!	What a day
( )	Mr Dot the teacher was eating his lunch.
" "	Get lost, boomed the man.
;	We couldn't be beaten it just couldn't happen.

Add an appropriate prefix.

	believe
	freeze
	plane
	paid
	charge
	fill
	usual

Add the capital letters, commas and full stops.

yesterday we went for lunch with mr johnson jenny and phillip

Circle subordinating conjunctions.

until	whether
regret	fool
although	since

SPaG SPOTTER

Circle the relevant part of speech.

Can you spot…?	Context
the nouns	The boys were playing football in the park with their friends.
the verbs	Clean up your room and help your sister with her homework.
the adjectives	The crumbling mountain couldn't support the delicate ecosystem.
the adverbs	Singing loudly, I was completely relaxed.
the articles	I would love to have a friend like you.
the determiner	If only I could find those comfortable slippers.
the prepositions	Jimmy was perched on the table while Alex hid under the table.
a coordinating conjunction	We were all ready to leave, but Fred had forgotten his bag.
the pronouns	She was so cool, I admired her so much.
a subordinating conjunction	Although it was late, Paul wanted to stay up to watch the film.
a noun phrase	I could see lots of yummy, cold yoghurt.

Edit the sentence to make it correct.

Can you add…?	Context
a comma to make a fronted adverbial	Even though she was tall I knew I could still beat her.
add commas in the list	Even Derek Gina Phillip and Mark were going to the party.
a / an	The class dearly wanted to adopt _____ elephant.
brackets	Mr Hill the class teacher was determined to beat the children.
the capital letters	underneath the manchester skyline, jenny could see mary crying.

  Vocabulary Ninja © Andrew Jennings, 2019

CUTS – CIRCLE, UNDERLINE, TICK, STATE

C.U.T.S requires pupils to answer questions by circling, underlining, ticking and stating their answers. Pupils must become acutely aware of the skill that a question demands, demonstrating their knowledge of the curriculum, but also an attention to detail within the instructions of a question.

All the question types make greater cognitive demands on pupils as they need to not only know the subject matter well enough to answer the question, but also ensure they follow the instructions found within the question. These are all key skills that might be needed in an exam and are important to rehearse.

Pupils will need a comprehensive understanding of all age-appropriate spelling, punctuation and grammar to complete the worksheets on the next two pages.

NINJA NOTES

Ensure pupils understand that if they select the correct answer but don't follow the instructions precisely, they won't receive a mark. #readcarefully #beninja

CUTS – CIRCLE, UNDERLINE, TICK, STATE

✂

Circle the nouns in the sentence below.

It was the day that the team had been waiting for; Ali, John and Pablo were finally ready to make their dreams come true.

Circle the prepositions in the sentence below.

As I walked through the city, I could see inside restaurants and watched people skirting around each other.

Underline the noun phrase in the sentence below.

I went to watch the amazing ballerina dance.

Tick the sentence which uses speech punctuation correctly.

"I just can't believe we left Neil behind" John said regretfully. ☐

John said regretfully, "I just can't believe we left Neil behind." ☐

Suggest three conjunctions to complete the sentences.

Dan wanted to play darts _____ paint a picture. Unfortunately, it was raining, _____ he decided to paint. Once it had finished raining he went outside, _____ it was too wet to play.

 Vocabulary Ninja © Andrew Jennings, 2019

CUTS – CIRCLE, UNDERLINE, TICK, STATE

Circle the adverbs in the sentences below.

Adrian's dog barked loudly and Jenny's dog barked too.

The children angrily chased after each other on the playground.

Circle the articles in the passage below.

Mrs Thompson visited the store. She needed to buy a few items. On her list was a bag of oranges, the latest football comic and an upside down cake.

Underline the subordinate clause the sentences below.

Although I already knew, we all acted surprised when mum arrived.

Tomorrow was the big day, if only it would come sooner.

Tick the sentence which uses speech punctuation correctly.

Anton, Leyla, Paul and Freddy all screamed, "Help!" ☐

Anton, Leyla, Paul and Freddy all screamed "Help!" ☐

Suggest three conjunctions to complete the sentences.

I could not bring myself to eat another cake, _____ could Chidi. We decided to clean up _____ we moved all of the plates _____ scraped them into the bin.

PICTURE PROCESSOR

The Picture processor processes and decodes an image into the SPaG that it is made up of. It is a fantastic visual resource and is provided with stimulus images so you can use it straightaway. Adapt the resource for your own class or topic by overlaying an image of your choice before you photocopy the resource. The Picture processor is underpinned by the power of three: in each section, the pupil is only allowed to add three items. In the case of this resource, less is more! Pupils have to finish off by pulling all of the processed words back together in the form of a detailed sentence.

Nouns – When you look at the image, whatever you can see is a noun!

Pronouns and noun phrases – Noun phrases are groups of words that revolve around a head word, the noun or possibly an indefinite pronoun.

Fronted adverbials – Fronted adverbials are groups of words that help to begin sentences in a more varied fashion. They tell us more about how, where, when, what, who and why. They can help add more detail to the sentence. A good way to create them is to look at the image, think about where the image is, what is happening, and what time of day it is.

Adjectives – The building blocks of any great sentence! Once adjectives have been mastered, ensure that pupils understand expanded noun phrases, that they can create them and identify them in other sentences. When you look at the image, how would you describe what you see?

Verbs – Pupils will need to think carefully about the tense they use in regards to the image they see. What is it that the subject or objects are being, doing or having?

Prepositions – Prepositions add even more detail to a sentence and can go unnoticed. For additional challenge, pupils should be shown how to create and identify prepositional phrases.

Adverbs – Adverbs can help the reader understand in greater detail *how* something is occurring. Often adverbs end in -ly, but not always! They are superb for bringing a sentence to life.

Sentence – The final task is to create a detailed sentence using some or all of the grammatical strands. To use them all, pupils will also need to be skilled at using commas and other punctuation to create multi-clause sentences.

Conjunctions – In the finished sentence, we will most likely only see one conjunction as not all conjunctions will suit the image. More able pupils should be thinking about subordinating conjunctions, rather than coordinating ones.

Determiners – Determiners help us determine noun groups, tense, quantity and possession.

Vocabulary Ninja © Andrew Jennings, 2019

PICTURE PROCESSOR

Look at this photograph for one minute. Discuss what you see with a partner, then make a list all of the words you have used to describe the photograph.

NINJA NOTE Use the power of three. You can only add three items to each box.

Nouns:	Adjectives:	Verbs:
Pronouns and noun phrases:	**Prepositions:**	**Adverbs:**
Fronted adverbials:	**Conjunctions:**	**Determiners:**

Sentence:
_____
_____
_____

PICTURE PROCESSOR

Look at this photograph for one minute. Discuss what you see with a partner, then make a list all of the words you have used to describe the photograph.

NINJA NOTE   Use the power of three. You can only add three items to each box.

Nouns:	Adjectives:	Verbs:
Pronouns and noun phrases:	**Prepositions:**	**Adverbs:**
Fronted adverbials:	**Conjunctions:**	**Determiners:**

Sentence:

VOCABULARY VAULT

In this chapter, you'll find vocabulary for close to 60 different topic areas linked to the National Curriculum. Vocabulary Ninja has identified significant figures, adjectives, verbs and nouns that will all support the writing process. An estimate of words in this section is approximately 50 different words per topic over 50 topics – that's 2000 different pieces of vocabulary ready for staff and pupils to use instantly!

VOCABULARY VAULT

Anglo-Saxons

Battle of Hastings	William the Conqueror	Nouns	Adjectives	Verbs
1066	Norman	Angle	resourceful	farm
arrow	Normandy	Saxon	versatile	scavenge
eye	superior	Jute	practical	weave
exhaustion	well-trained	Beowulf	adept	worship
conquered	crowned	farmer	creative	craft
France	invader	Sutton Hoo	violent	trade
Norway	castles	tapestry	aggressive	battle
Sussex	victorious	weaponry	skilled	attack
Senlac Hill	king	ship	bold	voyage
cavalry	famous	Mercia	marauding	entertain

Animals

Animals	Animals	Nouns	Adjectives	Verbs
elephant	wolf	horn	furry	whimper
giraffe	badger	paw	colourful	snarl
lion	meerkat	tusk	dangerous	swallow
rhinoceros	tortoise	snout	slithery	nibble
kangaroo	woodpecker	tentacle	stealthy	charge
orangutan	vulture	hump	camouflaged	crawl
whale	flamingo	antler	elegant	creep
octopus	kingfisher	flipper	poisonous	swoop
hippopotamus	shark	feather	strong	pounce
swordfish	jellyfish	venom	feathered	gnaw

VOCABULARY VAULT

Anne Frank

Anne	Camps	Nouns	Adjectives	Verbs
diary	concentration	sister	brave	invade
Jewish	Auschwitz	parent	anxious	forbid
persecuted	prison	World War	hidden	arrest
imprisoned	labour	religion	intelligent	evacuate
Bergen-Belsen	death	Jew	tragic	publish
secret-annex	torture	Margo	abhorrent	survive
arrested	conditions	Adolf Hitler	descriptive	liberate
Amsterdam	Holocaust	Kitty	worried	evade
Otto / Edith	millions	annex	fearful	defy
bookcase	deceit	Nazi	courageous	grieve

Capital cities

Cities	Cities	Nouns	Adjectives	Verbs
London	Cairo	museum	ancient	discover
Edinburgh	Tunis	art galleries	historic	explore
Cardiff	Kabul	river	beautiful	travel
Dublin	Bangkok	war	famous	build
Madrid	Seoul	culture	imperial	photograph
Rome	Bucharest	palace	metropolitan	speak
Paris	Beijing	landmark	vast	describe
Oslo	Brasilia	government	crowded	learn
Helsinki	Lima	tourism	flourishing	immerse
Zagreb	Buenos Aires	cathedral	thriving	create

VOCABULARY VAULT

Christopher Columbus

Columbus	Explorer	Nouns	Adjectives	Verbs
navigator	discover	King Ferdinand	adventurous	sail
explorer	find	sailor	bold	convince
sailor	search	voyager	rebellious	explore
Italian	explore	New World	innovative	settle
voyages	navigate	spices	naive	return
Americas	sail	gold	personable	build
East Indies	voyage	Spain	intelligent	capture
Indians	sickness	disease	famous	rescue
colonise	death	Santa Maria	dangerous	starve
exploit	indigenous	compass	historic	enslave

Climate zones

Polar	Temperate	Tropical	Desert	Weather
freezing	moderate	equator	no rainfall	blizzard
icy	four seasons	wet	The Sahara	storm
snow	variable	monsoon	dry conditions	torrential
below zero	Spring	rain forest	cactus	drought
Siberia	Summer	predictable	hibernate	flood
poles	Winter	floods	sand	temperature
inhospitable	inhabited	mud slides	heat	rainbow
Arctic	unpredictable	drought	cold	downpour
Antarctica	Europe	humid	camel	drizzle
penguin	London	insects	lizards	thermometer

Vocabulary Ninja © Andrew Jennings, 2019

VOCABULARY VAULT

Dinosaurs

T-Rex	Pterodactyl	Nouns	Adjectives	Verbs
lizard	pterosaur	extinction	deadly	discover
theropod	reptile	dinosaur	sluggish	scavenge
Cretaceous	carnivore	predator	agile	bite
tyrant	fish	carnivore	swift	roam
muscular	wings	food chain	primitive	stomp
aggressive	muscle / skin	herbivore	fearsome	evolve
predator	fingers	scales	magnificent	fly
short arms	unique	camouflage	beastly	hunt
scavenger	jagged beak	museum	colourful	forage
intelligent	recognisable	meteor	enormous	roar

Egyptians

Tutankhamun	H. Carter	Nouns	Adjectives	Verbs
boy-king	famous	mummy	mighty	mummify
malaria	explorer	hieroglyph	knowledgeable	entomb
entombed	archaeologist	cartouche	democratic	poison
frail	Egyptologist	River Nile	civilised	unearth
King Tut	excavated	pyramid	decadent	immortalise
excavated	wealthy	Giza	wealthy	embalm
deformed	artist	Sphinx	scientific	betray
mysterious	lymphoma	canopic jar	primitive	bribe
pharaoh	treasures	inscription	prosperous	invent
sarcophagus	historic	desert	intelligent	bicker

VOCABULARY VAULT

Electricity

Appliances	Key Words	Nouns	Adjectives	Verbs
iron	conductor	energy	tidal	open
television	insulator	turbine	solar	close
socket	open	power station	clean	surge
iPad	closed	motor	dirty	bridge
mobile phone	circuit	fossil fuel	cheap	observe
lamp	incomplete	current	renewable	resist
toaster	broken	voltage	nuclear	brighten
microwave	flow	battery	geothermal	light
hairdryer	resistance	pylon	dangerous	burn
speaker	static	ammeter	safety	investigate

Explorers

Captain Cook	Francis Drake	Nouns	Adjectives	Verbs
British	circumnavigate	pathfinder	illustrious	navigate
cartographer	Spanish	captain	audacious	transport
navigator	Armada	conditions	intrepid	explore
South Pacific	Atlantic	weather	resolute	discover
apprentice	New World	weapon	infamous	exchange
Royal Navy	victorious	route	adventurous	research
Endeavour	revenge	expedition	ardent	battle
healthy crew	pirate	merchant	curious	inspire
Whitby	privateer	trailblazer	wealthy	trade
Easter Island	The Dragon	ration	vast	traverse

VOCABULARY VAULT

Fairy tales

Red Riding Hood	Goldilocks	Nouns	Adjectives	Verbs
wolf	careless	princess	cruel	trick
help	chair	castle	deadly	touch
Grandma	porridge	bed	wooden	protect
cottage	three bears	forest	beautiful	believe
basket	sleepy	wolf	magical	befriend
cloak	beautiful	chair	loveable	climb
woodcutter	frustrated	kitchen	deformed	discard
devour	kitchen	axe	enchanted	smell
disguise	breakfast	cow	dangerous	disguise
rescue	wandered	harp	sneaky	chase

Famous women

Rosa Parks	Malala	Nouns	Adjectives	Verbs
activist	human rights	respect	heroic	enthuse
bus	Pakistan	legend	brave	stand
boycott	education	hardship	plucky	demonstrate
segregation	Islam	challenge	radical	protest
different	multilingual	story	enlightened	convince
NAACP	Taliban	pioneer	unwavering	defy
arrested	women	equality	unsung	accomplish
appeal	shot	adversity	valiant	survive
symbol	survivor	integrity	veracious	struggle
freedom	Nobel Peace	resilience	honest	persist

VOCABULARY VAULT

Florence Nightingale

Florence	Life and Work	Nouns	Adjectives	Verbs
nurse	training	heroine	kind	nurse
nursing	wounded	Russia	heroic	wash
Crimean War	diseases	Lady Lamp	thoughtful	clean
soldiers	death	patient	caring	challenge
famous	sickness	Scutari	courageous	revolutionise
hospital	injuries	Miss Smith	inspirational	impose
Crimea	cleaning	Florence	ambitious	train
Sidney Herbert	cleanliness	anaesthetic	loving	love
doctors	patients	museum	devoted	save
medicine	investigate	founded	selfless	rescue

Great Fire of London

London	Samuel Pepys	Nouns	Adjectives	Verbs
Thames	diary	Great Fire	raging	decimate
capital	British	bakery	smoky	demolish
medieval	government	houses	burning	smoke
narrow	Royal Navy	timber	consuming	extinguish
sanitation	Star Inn	gunpowder	damaging	damage
unhygienic	primary source	plague	blistering	spread
Pudding Lane	writing	drought	infernal	engulf
combustible	record	devastation	vicious	explode
population	first person	September	consuming	douse
common	detail	flame	hellish	record

VOCABULARY VAULT

Greeks

Zeus	Spartan	Nouns	Adjectives	Verbs
imposing	fitness	Hades	civilised	invade
immortal	military	Sparta	primitive	conquer
thunder	fearless	Zeus	united	honour
lightning	discipline	Hera	aristocratic	drape
titans	toughness	Xerxes	provocative	battle
Olympus	phalanx	Paris	ancient	preside
Hera	excellence	Archimedes	religious	defeat
mortals	Leonidas	Parthenon	cultural	sacrifice
revered	exercise	Mount Olympus	ruthless	encounter
merciful	rigorous	Aphrodite	artistic	crush

Gunpowder Plot

Guy Fawkes	Robert Catesby	Nouns	Adjectives	Verbs
gunpowder	leader	revenge	devious	survive
guarding	mastermind	battle	bloody	attempt
discovered	recruiter	conspirator	murderous	thwart
arrested	catholic	Parliament	horrific	assassinate
explosives	assassinate	London	repulsive	ignite
beneath	revolt	bonfire	organised	destroy
tortured	influential	November 5th	sneaky	conspire
patsy	shot	guard	illegal	prevent
cellars	letter	treason	tactical	hang
effigy	fled	barrel	infamous	murder

VOCABULARY VAULT

Habitats

Burrow	Nest	Dam	Polar	Adjectives
hole	birds	water	North Pole	vast
tunnel	laying eggs	barrier	South Pole	narrow
dig	safety	restrict	penguin	underground
hollow	height	flow	cold	damp
set	roost	stream	windy	fragile
den	shelter	reservoir	snow	solid
dwelling	construct	flood	tundra	murky
safety	hatching	river	polar bear	secure
retreat	twigs	floodgates	Artic	snug
earth	storage	irrigation	Antarctic	wild

Holocaust

Hitler	Heydrich	Nouns	Adjectives	Verbs
Auschwitz	high-ranking	antisemitism	bloody	execute
cruel	fearsome	Bergen-Belsen	ghastly	transport
criminal	iron-heart	death squads	callous	slaughter
holocaust	architect	Gestapo	unforgivable	cleanse
Fuhrer	deportation	gas chamber	wretched	escape
embroiled	authorised	Nazi	infamous	exterminate
invader	retribution	genocide	noxious	symbolise
vain	Himmler	children	calculated	murder
dictator	mastermind	women	cruel	imprison
racist	ruthless	Mein Kampf	nightmarish	deport

Vocabulary Ninja © Andrew Jennings, 2019

VOCABULARY VAULT

Human body

Skeleton	Organs	Nouns	Adjectives	Verbs
cranium	brain	nerves	muscular	regulate
mandible	heart	cell	physical	break down
sternum	lungs	carbon dioxide	obese	produce
femur	kidney	oxygen	magnificent	eat
fibula	liver	muscle	fragile	digest
tibia	intestine	bones	tall	remove
radius	bowel	pulse	rigid	transport
ulna	skin	ligament	breakable	circulate
patella	blood vessels	artery	vital	absorb
humerus	spinal cord	vein	overweight	breathe

Knights and castles

Knights	Castles	Nouns	Adjectives	Verbs
sword	stone	tower	metallic	applaud
shield	moat	chainmail	deadly	pillage
brave	defence	dragon	shimmering	destroy
loyal	protect	tournament	loyal	canter
well-trained	villagers	castle	dangerous	prevail
protector	drawbridge	helmet	wooden	honour
honour	gatehouse	squire	impassable	barrage
military	dungeon	gauntlet	heavy	fire
armour	courtyard	catapult	powerful	launch
horse	ramparts	jester	tough	provoke

VOCABULARY VAULT

Light

Isaac Newton	Eratosthenes	Nouns	Adjectives	Verbs
scientist	Alexandria	metal	colourful	measure
prism	library	wood	dark	appear
wave	geometry	battery	light	illuminate
spectrum	sciences	mirror	short	bounce
theory	Syene	source	long	reflect
particle	discovery	sun	faint	permeate
experiment	world	glass	translucent	distort
prove	sticks	shadow	artificial	absorb
beam	paper	light	partial	erupt
refract	water well	rainbow	opaque	create

London

Buildings	Places	Nouns	Adjectives	Verbs
Shard	River Thames	history	international	travel
London Eye	Hyde Park	culture	historic	visit
Buckingham	Covent Garden	airport	natural	guard
Palace	Camden Lock	bicycle	bustling	experience
Wembley	West End	parks	eclectic	march
Downing Street	London Zoo	music	rich	purchase
Big Ben	Westminster	tourist	inventive	observe
O2 Arena	Notting Hill	underground	cultured	explore
St. Paul's	China Town	tube	traditional	cycle
Cathedral	Greenwich	black cab	picturesque	ride

VOCABULARY VAULT

Mini-beasts

Earthworm	Ant	Nouns	Adjectives	Verbs
soil	strong insect	ecosystem	slimy	hibernate
slither	six legs	environment	abundant	consume
no legs	team	habitat	powerful	shelter
tunnel	social	insect	slithering	transform
replicate	colony	wings	predator	tunnel
sections	queen	exoskeleton	poisonous	pollinate
hermaphrodite	drone	mollusc	delicate	devour
moisture	forage	sting	smooth	scuttle
annelid	worker	grasshopper	rough	inject
decomposer	black / red	centipede	aggressive	crush

Mountains

Edmund Hillary	Mt. Everest	Nouns	Adjectives	Verbs
explorer	mountain	mountaineer	magnificent	ascend
first	highest	climber	sheer	prevail
influential	29,029ft	piste	imposing	perish
inspiration	Holy Mother	disaster	volcanic	endure
Himalayas	K2	Tenzing Norgay	inaccessible	climb
Khumbu Icefall	290 deaths	ascent	impassable	cripple
beekeeper	blizzard	record	beautiful	mount
summit	avalanche	peak	picturesque	conquer
Sherpa	base camp	weather	snow-capped	emaciate
humble	climbing	equipment	royal	persist

VOCABULARY VAULT

Natural disasters

Tsunami	Earthquake	Nouns	Adjectives	Verbs
earthquake	tectonic	geologist	catastrophic	collapse
seismic	aftershock	ocean	volatile	barrage
location	fault	fault lines	unstable	destroy
tidal wave	amplitude	hurricanes	appalling	restore
ocean	core	tornado	phenomenal	evacuate
deadly	tremor	volcano	chaotic	warn
flood	mantle	flood	violent	surge
underwater	crust	mud slides	unforeseen	tremble
debris	magnitude	storm	imminent	devastate
coastal	Richter Scale	death	menacing	grieve

On a farm

Animals	Vehicles	Nouns	Adjectives	Verbs
cow	tractor	farmer	muddy	open
horse	jeep	hatchery	smelly	close
sheep	car	vermin	disgusting	feed
sheep dog	van	fertiliser	loud	herd
bull	combine harvester	trough	noisy	gallop
pig	motorbike	stable	messy	shout
chicken	plough	manure	isolated	catch
rooster	hay baler	paddock	difficult	milk
mouse	cultivator	farmhouse	fertile	sell
goose	quad bike	tractor	tiring	groom

Vocabulary Ninja © Andrew Jennings, 2019

VOCABULARY VAULT

Pirates

John Silver	Pirate Ship	Nouns	Adjectives	Verbs
cunning	plank	eye-patch	dirty	plan
villain	Jolly Roger	flag	ruthless	sail
parrot	wooden	palm tree	dangerous	attack
one-legged	crow's nest	treasure	strong	plunder
crutch	overboard	gold	swashbuckling	board
disability	barrel	cannon	fearsome	parlay
fearsome	galleon	sea	golden	fight
courageous	first mate	shipwreck	jagged	navigate
infamous	cutlass	chest	scruffy	steal
silver	anchor	mast	lazy	drink

Plague

Doctors	Symptoms	Nouns	Adjectives	Verbs
demonic	buboes	sewage	epidemic	treat
spices	fever	fleas	rampant	endure
herbs	chills	plague	dreadful	transmit
overpower	pain	smoke	severe	infect
repel	vomiting	sanitation	profound	quarantine
evil	bleeding	exodus	unknown	destroy
protect	gangrene	London	infectious	kill
infection	blackening	swelling	contagious	prescribe
beak	headaches	remedy	chronic	imprison
rats	legions	streets	sudden	diagnose

VOCABULARY VAULT

Plants

Plants	Plants	Nouns	Adjectives	Verbs
flower	stigma	flower	scientific	unearth
leaf	style	garden	leafy	observe
stem	ovary	greenhouse	tolerant	protect
roots	sepal	seed	stunning	decompose
sun	stem	compost	green	water
water	filament	insect	fleshy	feed
grow	stamen	pollen	giant	aerate
seed	germinate	bucket	tolerant	create
weed	pollinate	tray	withered	bloom
leaves	photosynthesis	soil	fragrant	produce

Plastic pollution

Plastic	Affected	Danger	Adjectives	Verbs
bottle	sea birds	hazard	microscopic	protect
micro-bead	fish	pollutant	durable	clean
carrier bag	algae	pollution	useful	save
food wrapping	humans	damaging	nuisance	remove
flip flops	whales	toxic	impossible	recycle
straws	dolphins	debris	unsustainable	consume
balloon	crabs	suffocate	disgusting	gather
netting	turtles	starvation	preventable	educate
tyres	sea life	garbage	widespread	ingest
tubs and trays	everyone	infested	polluted	swallow

VOCABULARY VAULT

Potions

Wizard	Witch	Nouns	Adjectives	Verbs
beastly	monstrous	mixture	toxic	inject
bearded	gruesome	antidote	lethal	enchant
powerful	repugnant	cork	magical	combine
wise	pregnant	container	viscous	curse
insane	matted	vapour	enchanting	froth
wicked	feline	alchemist	powerful	blend
ancient	raspy	spell	secret	dissolve
legendary	serrated	sorcerer	poisonous	hex
powerful	cackle	charm	harmful	invent
staff	decayed	elixir	unsafe	transform

Rainforest

Orangutan	Tree Frog	Noun	Adjectives	Verbs
ape	amphibian	canopy	wondrous	cover
leaves	frog	layer	diverse	scavenge
insects	vibrant	habitat	mature	discover
mammal	sticky pads	reptiles	extensive	rain
bulky	foliage	mammals	remote	locate
solitary	insectivore	species	dangerous	evaporate
forager	rivers	oxygen	dense	reproduce
creative	ponds	nutrients	temperate	contain
intelligent	tadpole	plants	moist	adapt
endangered	vertebrate	eco-system	rotting	survive

VOCABULARY VAULT

Religious festivals

Ramadan	Diwali	Nouns	Adjectives	Verbs
Eid Al-Fitr	Hinduism	Islam	friendly	pray
fasting	festival	Muslim	colourful	share
Quran	light	Jesus	royal	eat
five pillars	lantern	Quran	historic	celebrate
sawm	Sikhism	Nian	welcoming	fast
zakat	Rama	tradition	inventive	illuminate
taraweeh	Sita	parade	traditional	forgive
salat	bindi	celebrate	loud	receive
prayer	diva lamp	prayer	noisy	gather
Islam	rangoli	decorations	crowded	help

Rivers

Thames	Nile	Noun	Adjectives	Verbs
London	Africa	source	microscopic	travel
bridges	Egypt	erosion	durable	purify
islands	6,695km	tide	useful	meet
London Eye	4,160 miles	sea	nuisance	engulf
346km	Mediterranean	dam	impossible	plunge
215 miles	longest	current	unsustainable	collect
pollution	fertile	mudflats	disgusting	erode
salty	lakes	river bank	preventable	deposit
capital	papyrus	stream	widespread	fill
North Sea	flood plain	meander	polluted	rise

 Vocabulary Ninja © Andrew Jennings, 2019

VOCABULARY VAULT

Romans

Caesar	Soldier	Nouns	Adjectives	Verbs
betrayed	well-trained	Rome	vicious	march
ruler	loyal	toga	ancient	rule
friend	fearless	empire	proud	plot
mastermind	skilled	slave	illustrious	execute
reckless	obedient	ballista	warlike	enslave
vain	iconic	chariot	wealthy	duel
ambitious	brutal	villa	infamous	betray
dictator	ruthless	gladius	primitive	skirmish
visionary	legionary	amphitheatre	mighty	bicker
assassinated	centurion	standard	decadent	backstab

Seaside

Wildlife	Beach	Noun	Adjectives	Verbs
seagull	sand	lifeguard	calm	paddle
crab	sandcastle	rock pool	glistening	relax
jellyfish	sun	dock	windswept	visit
fish	shell	boat	rocky	stroll
shrimp	bucket	shell	tropical	float
tadpole	space	donkey	golden	snack
starfish	hat	current	interesting	construct
mussels	dune	spade	calm	gallop
seal	pier	pebble	popular	play
puffin	shore	bucket	crowded	splash

VOCABULARY VAULT

Seasons

Spring	Summer	Autumn	Winter	Weather
March	June	September	December	blizzard
April	July	October	January	temperature
May	August	November	February	wildlife
buds	sunflower	leaves	ice	flood
lamb	lawnmower	rain	snowflakes	drought
egg	holiday	brown	jumper	vegetation
chick	beach	orange	gloves	foliage
blossom	park	red	snowman	warmth
rain	paddling	harvest	woolly hat	growth
grow	storms	foliage	snowman	hibernate

Space

Tim Peake	N. Armstrong	Planets	Adjectives	Verbs
pilot	Buzz Aldrin	Mercury	lunar	launch
expedition	astronaut	Venus	bold	orbit
military	engineer	Earth	regimented	land
European	moon	Mars	distant	pilot
Space	pilot	Jupiter	perilous	breathe
Agency	lunar module	Saturn	unknown	propel
training	Eagle	Uranus	freezing	navigate
triathlon	commander	Neptune	profound	communicate
spacewalk	splashdown	meteor	historic	train
father	humble	Moon	breath-taking	eclipse

VOCABULARY VAULT

Stone Age

Neanderthal	Mammoth	Nouns	Adjectives	Verbs
caveman	tusk	spear	beastly	shelter
primitive	hunted	weapon	thundering	destroy
bone	clothing	civilisation	unintelligent	hunt
hunter	weapons	survival	lethal	cook
gatherer	dangerous	glacier	primitive	survive
shelter	deadly	shelter	rugged	track
forest	enormous	evolution	natural	forage
artwork	extinct	nomad	fertile	gather
tribe	forager	Neanderthal	filthy	skin
Skara Brae	extinct	artefact	tenacious	evolve

Suffragettes

Suffragette	E. Pankhurst	Noun	Adjectives	Verbs
movement	leader	Emily Davison	violent	vote
protest	political	women	radical	strike
politics	activist	union	persistent	handcuff
suffrage	strong	sympathy	selfless	transcend
vote	imprisoned	martyr	determined	suffer
campaign	persuade	election	willing	trigger
equal	contributor	rights	unwavering	spur
opportunities	legacy	suffrage	intense	perpetuate
fighting	significant	labour	militant	battle
tactical	selfless	King's horse	violent	endure

VOCABULARY VAULT

Superheroes

Spiderman	Batman	Superman	Wonder Woman	Mindset
Peter Parker	Bruce Wayne	Clark Kent	Diana Prince	intelligent
climb	utility belt	Lois Lane	Amazonian	brave
web	batmobile	Daily Planet	Themyscira	tactical
bite	lair	kryptonite	shield	determined
venom	sidekick	Krypton	Lasso of Truth	selfless
agility	Robin	cape	sword	energetic
senses	Alfred	fly	Ares	fearless
spider	Gotham City	Lex Luther	armour	isolated
arachnid	villains	reporter	bracelets	generous
teenager	orphan	glasses	boomerang	courageous

The Maya

Conquistador	Warrior	Noun	Adjectives	Verbs
Spanish	well-trained	Armada	ambitious	invent
metallic	loyal	art	primitive	fight
armoured	fearless	Maya	outstanding	observe
powerful	indigenous	trade	exceptional	destroy
smallpox	tribes	maize	deadly	infect
firearms	lifetime	medicine	educated	observe
artillery	training	Chichen-Itza	greedy	trick
animals	head-dress	warrior	ruthless	defend
tactics	savage	ceramics	naive	sacrifice
warfare	animal pelt	astronomy	sophisticated	abandon

VOCABULARY VAULT

Titanic

Edward Smith	Sinking	Nouns	Adjectives	Verbs
Captain	Southampton	death	infamous	save
perished	New York	collision	glorious	collide
White Star Line	iceberg	merchant	luxurious	float
SS Celtic	North Atlantic	passenger	foundering	survive
Baltic	2,224 on board	life vest	horror	inflate
Adriatic	lifeboats	iceberg	broad	obliterate
Olympic	collision	wreck	unsinkable	gouge
adversity	starboard	disaster	spacious	breach
hero	1500 died	tragedy	doomed	freeze
immersed	ill-prepared	superliner	regal	die

Toys

Victorian	Modern	Noun	Adjectives	Verbs
yo-yo	tablet	blow football	new	play
pop gun	Lego	Atari	fun	flick
whip and top	Hatchimals	train set	old	move
cup and ball	Nintendo	Twister	colourful	touch
Jacob's ladder	Xbox	tiddlywinks	interesting	bounce
marbles	trading cards	Etch-a-Sketch	handmade	remember
wooden blocks	scooter	He-Man	musical	love
hopscotch	Paw Patrol Toys	Care Bear	stuffed	laugh
doll's house	fidget spinner	pogo stick	beautiful	argue
rocking horse	Transformers	Barbie	expensive	score

VOCABULARY VAULT

Tudors

Henry VIII	Wives	Nouns	Adjectives	Verbs
strong	Catherine of Aragon	gallows	ruthless	marry
athletic	Anne Boleyn	hood	insolent	joust
sportsman	Jane Seymour	Beefeater	promiscuous	behead
tennis	Anne of Cleves	executioner	elegant	execute
jousting	Katherine Howard	peasant	lustful	break-up
educated	Katherine Parr	Francis Drake	talented	abolished
Latin	divorced	gargoyle	attractive	widowed
obesity	beheaded	chemise	playful	divorce
charismatic	executed	banquet	jealous	tax
insecure	survived	scythe	turbulent	murder

Victorians

Queen Victoria	C. Darwin	Noun	Adjectives	Verbs
monarch	scientist	dunce cap	oppressive	explore
1837 - 1901	theory	mangle	dirty	diagnose
cousin married	evolution	steam engine	literary	maintain
9 children	HMS Beagle	marbles	impressive	overcrowd
author	specimen	science	enlightened	design
artist	voyage	washboard	polluted	pioneer
languages	animal	chalk	eloquent	teach
penny black	plant	cane	loving	dwell
Victoria Cross	study	factory	sporty	employ
jubilee	botany	camera	prosperous	manufacture

VOCABULARY VAULT

Vikings

Rollo	Erik the Red	Warrior	Adjectives	Verbs
leader	red hair	fierce	murderous	intimidate
raids	hot temper	honour	horrific	invade
France	banished	raider	enraged	exploit
9th century	manslaughter	monks	ruthless	unleash
Normandy	explorer	Valhalla	intelligent	navigate
invasion	settler	cultured	unkempt	settle
protector	colonist	burial	intrepid	capture
descendants	untamed	long ship	destructive	voyage
voyage	founder	Karl and Jarl	tactical	conquer
giant	killer	myths	rough	stalk

Volcanoes

Mt. St. Helens	Mt. Vesuvius	Mt. Etna	Adjectives	Verbs
4,400ft	4,190ft	10,922ft	intense	eject
Washington State	famous	Sicily	volcanic	scorch
USA	infamous	Italy	infernal	plume
monument	active	active	dangerous	choke
Skamania	Italy	rich soil	ferocious	spiral
County	Naples	tourism	mesmeric	smother
active	Pompeii	Mongibello	formidable	overwhelm
avalanche	79 AD	popular	colossal	explode
destruction	Herculaneum	sleeping	cataclysmic	burn
disaster	stratovolcano	monster	unstoppable	shatter

VOCABULARY VAULT

Water cycle

Water Cycle	Water Cycle	Nouns	Adjectives	Verbs
water	evaporation	mountain	peaceful	monitor
rain	transpiration	stream	frozen	trap
roots	precipitation	rain	muddy	cycle
sun	condensation	flood	natural	return
wind	filter	weather	relaxing	condense
snow	run-off	wildlife	wondrous	precipitate
lake	collection	tributaries	mighty	meander
river	transport	lake	narrow	pour
sea	storage	cycle	broad	flow
evaporation	atmosphere	ocean	dry	rise

World War I

Lloyd George	Wilhelm II	Noun	Adjectives	Verbs
Prime Minister	Emperor	RAF	inhuman	murder
solicitor	King	USSR	nightmarish	negotiate
opposed	abdicated	Great War	nauseating	persecute
conscription	ineffective	Germany	emotional	revenge
mediate	fled	Austria	cowardly	execute
frustrated	Erb's palsy	U-boat	fatal	survive
Allies	exile	Bully Beef	murderous	bomb
strategic	Prussia	France	loathsome	defend
appeasement	shocked	RMS Lusitania	bloody	invade
charming	Third Reich	battlefield	heroic	lead

ENTHRALLING ETYMOLOGY

This is a whole chapter dedicated to etymology and words that have interesting etymological stories to engage learners! Each of the words has a strong link to different parts of the curriculum. Plus, you'll find a bank of ideas about how to teach or use them in your already crammed curriculum.

Etymology was one of those words that was bandied around when I was an NQT. I would nod encouragingly in conversations but not really have any idea what it was. Etymology, in fact, is pretty awesome and is simply a scary name for something that is relatively straightforward: the study of where words came from.

The table on pages 99-105 has almost 100 pertinent words for pupils to explore. All of these words have been chosen to link with topics across the curriculum. One of the great things about lots of them is that they have some fabulously interesting stories behind them. The next few pages contain a wealth of ideas about how you might integrate the enthralling etymology strips into a lesson or your daily routine.

NINJA GAME 1: SPEAKING AND LISTENING SLIPS

Speaking and listening opportunities can be hard to come by, especially in the middle of a busy English or science lesson. Using etymology slips can be a great way to provide a simple yet informative etymological speaking and listening opportunity.

Prepare: Simply pre-print a page of etymology explanations and slice them up, keeping the word and its definition together. Place the strips in an envelope and pin it onto your working wall.

Pounce: Whenever you have a spare two minutes or an opportunity to fill, ask pupils to pick a ninja word from the envelope and read it aloud to the rest of the class. This is a perfect assessment opportunity, but more importantly, their word pool is now a little deeper.

NINJA GAME 2: MATCHING

Matching is a skill in itself and is especially important within reading comprehension. Pupils need to be able to match a word to its definition – quite simple really, or is it?

Prepare: Print a page and choose up to five words and associated explanations. Trim the word from the explanation about the origin of the word.

Pounce: First, present the words to the learners without the etymology. Ask them to hypothesise about the meaning of the word – what do they know about it already? Can they hear a root word held within it that might help them explain the word? All of this hypothesising will make the matching process much simpler. Now give the children the definitions. Can they match them together correctly? Alternatively, can you give the children the explanations first with the target word blanked out. Then ask the children to hypothesise about what the word might be.

NINJA GAME 3: HANDWRITING

In a busy classroom environment, it's hard to fit everything in. Why not use etymology slips to teach the etymology of words *and* develop pupils' handwriting skills? Rather than simple copying worksheets, this is a meaningful handwriting activity that expands vocabulary.

Prepare: Print the etymology strips. Trim the slips and distribute them to pupils. To add an extra level of learning, give each table a different word and have pupils orally share the etymology with their peers. This creates an additional speaking and listening opportunity.

Pounce: Ask pupils to copy their word into their exercise books as neatly as they can. Ensure pupils have the chance to lay their books open, creating a handwriting gallery. Encourage pupils to move around and feedback to each other about the handwriting styles. To add an additional focus, be explicit about the handwriting element you want pupils to focus on, such as ascenders and descenders being formed correctly.

NINJA GAME 4: TOPIC WORK

The majority of the etymology entries that have been provided have strong links to the primary National Curriculum, so they're perfect for topic and foundation subject lessons.

Prepare: Identify the vocabulary that supports your chosen topic and be ready to introduce it to the children.

Pounce: Use a relevant word and its etymology as a starter to each topic lesson. Have the etymology of the chosen word displayed on your interactive whiteboard or wall display and share it with the children. Think about how you can record this in a way that adds value. Could you have topic etymology books, where pupils record the etymology of the words? Why not finish with a quiz at the end of the year? Why not embed ICT skills? Have the pupils create an etymology blog that can be posted on the school's website or social media!

NINJA GAME 5: ILLUSTRATE AN ETYMOLOGY FLOOR BOOK

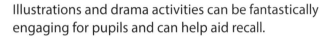

Illustrations and drama activities can be fantastically engaging for pupils and can help aid recall.

Prepare: I don't need to tell you about setting up a drawing activity, but we need to think about how we record this fantastic activity. Sometimes it won't be appropriate to record this in your foundation subject books.

Pounce: A great solution to this is to create a scrapbook or floor book and create a page for each word that you introduce to your class. Drop the etymology onto the page, then add examples of pupils' illustrations and thoughts about the word etymology itself.

NINJA GAME 6: GREEN SCREEN

This is another fabulous opportunity for speaking and listening and the associated assessment. Green screens quickly engages pupils and are an effective medium for sharing the pupils' learning. Have pupils present the new information as a news report with a superimposed image that is related to the etymology of the chosen word.

Prepare: First, you will require a tablet or smartphone that can download a green screen recording app. There are several simple yet effective ones available for free. For a small fee, you can access versions with more features to enhance the outcomes. Second, you will need a wall space where you can hang green cloth or even cover the wall in green backing paper. It helps if this area is fairly well lit.

Pounce: Once you have the area prepared and familiarised yourself with the app, you are ready to go. Just make sure the pupils aren't wearing green too! Display an image that illustrates the target word and its etymology, and invite the children to present their new learning.

NINJA GAME 7: FIVE-SENTENCE STORY

Five-sentence stories can be extremely entertaining and can provide a great insight into pupils' strengths in writing. Five-sentence stories are exactly what you might think they are: stories that are limited to five sentences. They can take the structure of your traditional story mountain and be as simple or as complex as a child can make them. Just add imagination.

Prepare: Modelling your very own five-sentence story would be a great place to start, showing the pupils exactly what you expect, using the etymology of the new word as an inspiration for the story. For example, if you have just introduced the etymology of the word 'buccaneer', that would be a great inspiration for a pirate or adventure story around Caribbean islands.

Pounce: Ask the children to create their own five-sentence stories using an etymology as inspiration.

NINJA GAME 8: TELL-A-TEACHER CHALLENGE

The tell-a-teacher challenge is a fabulous tool for spreading knowledge and understanding, which encourages pupils to use their communication skills with other adults.

Prepare: Introduce the new etymology to the children, then set the mission. 'Your mission, if you choose to accept it, is to tell as many adults in the school during break and lunch about the etymology of this new word! Good luck.'

Pounce: Model some of the language that pupils might use, e.g. 'Excuse me Miss/Sir, do you know the etymology of the word buccaneer?' This will give pupils the confidence to approach other adults across the school. It would be prudent to inform your colleagues that pupils will be approaching staff to share their new learning. Who can tell the most adults during break and lunch?

NINJA GAME 9: THE LITTLE BOOK OF ETYMOLOGY

A small book of enormous words! Decide whether you want to create a whole-class book or individual pupil books. Personally, I think individual books have a more intimate feel.

Prepare: Give pupils small books or booklets. Invite them to decorate them or even back them in wallpaper (very 90s).

Pounce: Every time you introduce a new etymology to the children, ask them to record the entry in their Little Book of Etymology. They could add images, definitions, associated topics and even sketches to bring the etymology to life.

ENTHRALLING ETYMOLOGY

Word	Etymology
Amazon	From the Greek *Amazones* (a tribe of war fighting women) who were dangerous and brutal. As you can imagine, the Amazon River isn't for the faint hearted!
armada	'Fleet of warships', from Medieval Latin *armata* meaning 'armed force'. The Spanish Armada was the allegedly invincible fleet sent by Philip II of Spain to defeat England in 1588.
artery	This word comes from the Latin and Greek word *arteria*, which means 'windpipe'. The arteries were originally thought to carry air throughout the body.
assassin	Members of a fanatical Muslim sect during the Crusades used to smoke hashish and then murder leaders on the opposing side. They started going by the name 'hashishiyyin' and through centuries of mispronunciation, English arrived at this word.
battery	This word originates from Old French *baterie*, meaning 'beating, thrashing, assault'. In the 1550s the French began to use the word describe artillery units, which discharged explosives towards the enemy walls. In the same sense, during the 1790s, it began to mean 'electrical cell' created by Benjamin Franklin, which discharged electricity much like the artillery.
berserk	This word, in its literal Scandinavian sense, is a 'raging warrior of superhuman strength'.
bonfire	This word has an uncertain past, although most people concede that it has an original meaning of 'bone fire'.
boycott	This word comes from when Captain Charles C. Boycott (1832-1897) refused to lower the rent for his tenant farmers. This was quickly adopted by newspapers in many languages, even as far as Japan 'boikotto'.
breakfast	This is usually the first meal of the day. During the night your body is considered to be in a mode called 'fasting' or in a 'fast'. You might 'break' or stop your fast in the morning.
bubo	This word means 'inflamed swelling in the glands' and originates from the 14th century and the bubonic plague.
buccaneer	This word emerged in the 17th century, originating from the French word *boucanier*, which meant 'a pirate; a curer of wild meats, a user of a *boucan*', a native grill for roasting meat.
burrow	Meaning a 'hole in the ground dug by an animal as a refuge or to live in', the word stems from *borewe* which comes from Old English *burgh* meaning a 'stronghold or fortress'.
bus	Originally an abbreviation of *omnibus*, meaning 'four-wheeled public vehicle with seats for passengers'.
careless	This word is an old English word meaning 'unconcerned'.

ENTHRALLING ETYMOLOGY

Word	Etymology
carnation	Most people, when they think of this word, picture a flower. But before it was used to describe a flower, it was used to refer to the pink colour of skin.
caterpillar	From the Middle English *piller* 'plunderer', from Late Latin *catta pilosa*, where *catta* meant 'hairy, shaggy, covered with hair'.
centipede	Venomous, many-legged, insect-sized arthropod, from French *centipède*, from Latin *centipeda* 'many-footed arthropod', from *centum* 'hundred' and *ped* meaning 'foot', so literally meaning 100 feet.
checkmate	This term, beloved by chess grand masters, comes from the Arabic *shah mat*, meaning 'the king died' or the Persian *shah mat*, meaning 'the king is helpless'.
chocolate	The Nahuatl *xocolatl* is made up of the parts *xococ*, meaning 'bitter', and *atl*, meaning 'water'.
clue	This word means 'anything that serves as a guide or aid in a task or problem'. According to Greek mythology, when Theseus entered the Labyrinth to kill the minotaur (a half-man, half-bull), he unraveled a 'clew' (a ball of string) behind him, so he could find his way back.
codpiece	A bagged appendage to the front of close-fitting breeches, from Old English *codd* 'a bag, pouch, husk' which in Middle English came to mean 'testicle'.
conspire	From Old French *conspirer*, from Latin meaning literally 'to breathe together'.
courage	This word is similar to 'bravery'. It is from the Old French word *curage*, which draws from the word *cuer*, meaning 'heart'.
cure	From Old French *curer* and Latin *curare* 'take care of', hence in medical language 'to treat'.
cycle	From Greek *kyklos* meaning 'circle, wheel, any circular body, circular motion or cycle of events'.
daisy	The flower. This word is actually a contraction of 'day's eye' because the flower opens in the morning and closes at night!
dam	Meaning 'barrier across a stream of water to obstruct its flow and raise its level', this word is probably from Old Norse *dammr* or Middle Dutch *dam*. Reinforced by Old English verb *fordemman* meaning 'to stop up, block'.
dandelion	From Old French *dent de lion* 'lion's tooth' (from its toothed leaves).
diary	From Latin *diarium* meaning 'daily allowance'. All origins and derivatives seem to relate to 'day', showing that an entry was to be made daily.
dinosaur	This word was coined in Modern Latin by Sir Richard Owen, from Greek *deinos* 'terrible' plus *sauros* 'lizard'. The word is sometimes used to describe 'a person or institution not adapting to change'.

ENTHRALLING ETYMOLOGY

Word	Etymology
disaster	This word comes from the Greek *dis* meaning 'bad', and *astron*, meaning 'star'. The Ancient Greeks used to blame calamities on unfavourable planetary positions.
eavesdrop	This word means 'to lurk near a place to hear what is said inside'. It comes from Old English *yfesdrype* 'place around a house where the rainwater drips off the roof'.
echo	This word means 'a sound repeated by reflection'. In classical mythology, there was a mountain nymph who was punished with a speech problem that meant she could only repeat the words of others.
erupt	This word originally came about in relation to the breakout of diseases. It comes from Latin *eruptus* meaning 'to break out, burst'. For volcanoes, the Latin word was actually used when talking about Mount Etna.
extinct	This word means 'extinguished, quenched', from Latin *extinctus/exstinctus*, meaning 'to put out, quench; go out, die out; kill, destroy'. It is commonly used to describe a species of animal that has died out.
extinguish	From Latin *extinguere* meaning to 'quench or put out (what is burning)'. From *ex-* for 'out' and *stinguere* for 'quench'.
factory	This word is a place where different processes are done or objects are made. The related word *factor* in Latin meant a 'doer or maker'.
flood	An Old English *flōd* was 'a flowing of water, tide, an overflowing of land by water, a deluge, Noah's Flood; mass of water, river, sea, wave'. In early modern English, it was often called a *floud*. In figurative use it can mean, 'a great quantity, a sudden abundance'.
genocide	A term used to describe violence against members of a national, ethnical, racial or religious group with the intent to destroy the entire group. The word was apparently coined in 1944 in reference to Nazi extermination of Jews, literally 'killing a tribe', from Greek *genos* 'race, kind' and *-cide* 'a killing'.
geography	'The science of description of the earth's surface', from Greek *geographia*, 'description of the earth's surface' from *geo-* meaning 'earth' and *-graphia* meaning 'description'.
ghoul	A legendary evil spirit that robs graves and feeds on corpses. The word comes from *ghūl* (which is itself from *ghāla*, meaning 'to seize').
glacier	This word is from Old French *glace*, meaning 'ice'.
greenhouse	This word is called this simply because it is a transparent house and all of the produce within is normally green.
groggy	This word means 'drunk, overcome with grog'. The word *grog* originated in the 18th century when a British Admiral was nicknamed 'Old Grog' because he wore a cloak made of *grogram*. The Admiral made sailors dilute their rum with water to make a mixture called *grog*.

ENTHRALLING ETYMOLOGY

Word	Etymology
hammer	Originally meaning 'stone tool', this word comes from Old English *hamor*.
hamstring	This word means 'the tendon at the back of the knee'. When the thighs of pigs (hams) were hung by butchers, they were hung through the string-like tendons of these muscles.
hazard	This word means 'danger or risk'. It comes from Old French *hasard*, *hasart* meaning 'game of chance played with dice'.
hero	This word means 'a man of superhuman strength or physical courage' and has close links to *hērōs* (Greek) meaning 'demi-god'.
hippopotamus	This word literally means 'river horse' in Greek. It might not look much like a horse, but it certainly lives in rivers.
holocaust	The word comes from the Greek word *holokauston* which refers to an animal sacrifice that is offered to a god in which the whole animal is completely burnt. Later it came to denote a massacre of large numbers of people.
hopscotch	This is a well-known children's game. The word combines *hop* and *scotch*, which means 'scratch', from the lines scored in the dirt to make the squares for the game.
hospital	This word comes from Late Latin *hospitale* 'guest-house, inn'. The meaning became 'institution for sick or wounded people' in the 1540s.
inspire	This word comes from *enspiren* meaning 'to fill (the mind, heart with grace)' and before that from Latin *inspirare* meaning 'blow into or breathe upon'.
Kilimanjaro	This is a mountain in Tanzania, Africa. It may originate from Swahili *kilima*, meaning '(little) mountain'.
knight	This word comes from Old English *cniht* meaning 'boy, youth, servant'. As time passed, this work became closely linked to a military servant or follower of the king. Finally it become a noble rank in the 16th century.
ladybird	This word originated in Britain where the insects became known as Our Lady's Bird instead of 'ladybug' as they were known elsewhere. 'Lady' means Mary, so these insects were Mary's birds/bugs.
lemur	The animal received its name from Latin. In Roman mythology, the plural 'lemures' was used to describe the evil spirits of the dead.
London	This word appeared in Latin as *Londinium*. By the first century CE, this was a commercial centre in Roman Britain.
Luftwaffe	This German word literally means 'air-weapon'. Th first part, *Luft*, is linked to 'loft', meaning go high in the air.
lunatic	This word is from Late Latin *lunaticus* meaning 'moon-struck'. This originated from the belief that insanity is caused by changes of the moon!

ENTHRALLING ETYMOLOGY

Word	Etymology
malaria	Most would associate this word with Africa, but it originates from Italy. It combines *mal* 'bad' and *aria* 'air', so it literally means 'bad air'. The term was used to describe the unpleasant air emanating from the marshlands of Rome, which was believed to cause the disease.
Matterhorn	One of the world's most famous mountains, has taken its name from its surroundings and appearance. *Matte* in German meaning 'meadow, pastureland' and *horn* from its horn-like shape.
million	A mathematical word for you to think about. From Italian *milione* meaning 'a great thousand'. It is interesting to note that the ancient Greeks didn't have a name for a number larger than ten thousand, and the Romans for none higher than a hundred thousand.
Mississippi	This is now the name of a state, but originally it was the name of the river running through it. The word comes from the French rendering of an Algonquian name meaning 'big river'; compare Ojibwa *mshi-* 'big' and *ziibi* 'river'.
moat	This word originated from the French *mote* meaning a 'hillock, mound or embankment' – quite the opposite of what we consider to be a moat today! In Norman times the meaning shifted when ditches were dug around castles to protect them.
mortgage	This word comes from the Old French *mort* 'dead' and *gage* 'pledge', and now I don't want to buy a house anymore!
naughty	This word originally meant 'having nothing', from *nought* and *-y*, but was also used to describe people having no morals.
nemesis	Today this word means mortal enemy. It is also the name of the Greek goddess who took revenge against those who showed arrogance before the gods.
orangutan	This word for an animal comes from the Malay *orang*, meaning 'person', and *hutan*, meaning 'forest' – so 'man of the forest'.
periscope	Viewing apparatus on a submarine, 1899, formed in English from *peri* meaning 'around' and *-scope* meaning 'instrument for viewing'. So the word means 'an instrument for looking around'.
phobia	This word means 'irrational fear, horror, aversion' and comes from Greek *phobos*. Phobos is the son of the Greek god Ares.
pirate	This word comes from Latin *pirata* meaning 'sailor, sea robber'.
plastic	From the 1630s, this word means 'capable of shaping or molding', from Latin *plasticus*, from Greek *plastikos* meaning 'able to be molded, pertaining to molding, fit for molding'.
protect	This word comes from the Latin *protectus,* past participle of *protegere*. The word is made of *pro* meaning 'before' and *tegere* meaning 'to cover'.

ENTHRALLING ETYMOLOGY

Word	Etymology
Pterodactyl	An extinct flying reptile. This word comes originally from Greek *pteron* 'wing' and *daktylos* 'finger'.
python	This word is the name of the enormous dragon-like serpent that was slain by the legendary hero Apollo. The site of its death was known as *Pytho* to the Ancient Greeks.
quarantine	This word used to mean the 'period a ship suspected of carrying disease is kept in isolation', from Italian *quarantina giorni*, literally 'space of forty days'. During the days of the Black Death, ships suspected of carrying the plague were not allowed to enter Venetian ports for a period of 40 days.
ransack	From the Old Norse *rannsaka* 'to pillage', literally 'search the house' (especially legally, for stolen goods).
rhinoceros	This word literally means 'nose-horned', from Greek *rhinokeros* where *rhinos* means 'nose' and *keras* means 'horn of an animal.
Russia	Vikings who travelled east and settled in Kiev in the ninth century were known as *Rus*.
salary	The word salary comes from the Latin *salarium*, said to be a soldier's allowance for the purchase of salt. In ancient times, salt was used for many important things, and was referred to as white gold. Used as antiseptic, a preservative and as payment.
sarcasm	It is descended ultimately from the late Greek *sarkasmos* 'a sneer, jest, taunt, mockery', from *sarkazein* literally 'to strip off the flesh'.
segregate	From Latin *segregare* meaning to 'set apart, lay aside; isolate; divide', literally 'separate from the flock'.
shark	A large fish with lots of varieties, e.g. great white and hammerhead. The origin of the name for these animals is under some debate, but the English word may be from a Mayan word, *xoc*. Northern Europeans seem not to have been familiar with these animals before voyages to the tropics began.
shelter	This word is possibly an alteration of Middle English *sheltron*, *sheldtrume* meaning 'roof or wall formed by locked shields'. You can imagine soldiers holding shields aloft in the air, joined together to protect the group from arrows or other enemy attacks.
shield	This word comes from the Old English *scield* meaning 'protect, defence' and in a more literal sense 'board'.
shrapnel	This word was the surname of a general who invented a type of exploding, fragmenting shell when he was a lieutenant in the Royal Artillery during the Peninsular War. These days the word is sometimes used to refer to small change in purses or pockets.

ENTHRALLING ETYMOLOGY

Word	Etymology
snail	This word essentially is a diminutive form of Old English *snaca* 'snake', which literally means 'creeping thing'.
sniper	Another word for a sharpshooter. This word was used by British soldiers in 1773 India to describe shooting from a hidden place. It is a reference to hunting snipe (a type of small bird) as game.
sunflower	It is suggested this flower was given its name due to its similarity to the sun itself!
Thames	This is the name for the river running through London. It is thought that the name comes from Old English *Temese*, from Latin *Tamesis* (51 B.C.E.), from British *Tamesa*, an ancient Celtic river name perhaps meaning 'the dark one'.
Thursday	The fifth day of the week. The name for this day stems from Old English *þurresdæg*, literally 'Thor's Day', who was the Norse god of thunder.
titanic	This word is derived from the word *titan* meaning 'gigantic, colossal'. The word was the name of a British passenger liner which sank in 1912, and the word became symbolic of the destruction of supposedly indestructible.
tsunami	This word is from Japanese – *tsu* 'harbor' and *nami* 'waves'.
typhoon	There are a few fascinating possible stories for this word. One favourite is from Greek *typhon*, meaning 'whirlwind'. It was personified as a father of the winds, a giant. Interestingly, the Arabic word *al-tufan* appears many times in the Koran to mean 'a flood or storm'.
Tyrannosaurus Rex	A large, carnivorous dinosaur that walked on two legs. Its name is from the Greek *tyrannos* 'tyrant' and *sauros* 'lizard', and the Latin *rex* 'king'.
Victoria	This woman's name means 'victory in war' in Latin, and is the name of the Roman goddess of victory.
volcano	This word stems from the name Vulcan, the Roman God of fire. The Romans actually believed that Vulcan's workshop was based at the foot of Mt. Etna.
whipping-boy	In Tudor times, wealthy families would often pay for a 'whipping-boy' if their child misbehaved. The whipping-boy received physical punishment instead of the rich child!
window	Translated literally from Old Norse, this word means 'wind eye'. It stems from *vindauga*, where *vindr* means *wind* and *auga* is *eye*.

SCINTILLATING SYNONYMS

Understanding synonyms can be a terrific way of expanding pupils' vocabulary, developing their spelling, punctuation and grammar knowledge and can help refine the incisiveness of their writing. As we have discussed earlier in the book, pupils can only use the words they hold within their working vocabulary, which is influenced by their environment. For nearly every pupil, the three environments they are exposed to are: home, school and unstructured environments.

The three models opposite illustrate the effect that social factors can have on the width and depth of a pupil's vocabulary. Pupils who have enriched experiences in all three environments are much more likely to have a more expansive vocabulary that filters through all aspects of their lives. The central part of each model is the vocabulary that is deeply embedded – vocabulary that pupils can draw upon and use effectively within any environment.

Notice the dashed external boundary to our vocabulary pool. Within the rich model, our word pools are being forced to expand as our environments expose us to more rich and varied language experiences. However, within the impoverished model, pupils' word pools aren't necessarily expanding, and they also have the potential to recede. The embedded language that is cross-environmental is also limited. Within this model, we can see how the school environment is crucial, and, in most instances, it is the only environment we can reasonably expect to control.

We want to ensure, where possible, that pupils' working oral and written vocabularies are expanding, growing and deepening at all times. As Vocabulary Ninjas, we can ensure that this happens for all pupils. It's logical to expect that for those pupils whose home and social environments are stimulating and enriched, that their experimental and embedded word pools will be growing at a much quicker rate. The rich/poor model illustrates the school environment as an enriched one. Yes, the pupils still have limited rich language experiences outside of the school environment, but school can make the difference – you can make the difference. For these pupils, the school environment is fighting the great fight, pushing and expanding the external boundary on its own. It's tough going it alone, but if the school environment doesn't do it, who will?

So, let's look at how synonyms can be the infantry troops of our word army, as we try to expand our environmental territories and take over the world! (Wait…did I say that last part out loud?)

DEVELOPING LONG-TERM VOCABULARY SKILLS

Synonyms can be made as simplistic or complex as required. The potential danger with synonyms is that they can be used in an extremely superficial manner if you don't dedicate the time to embedding pupils' understanding. The classic example of this can be found in an episode of *Friends* (the popular television sitcom from the 90s). Joey, one of the main characters, is trying to write a letter but is not competent enough to do so, and so is introduced to the thesaurus facility on his computer. He proceeds to swap out nearly every word in his letter for 'better' one with disastrous, yet hilarious, consequences. This is a terrific proxy for how synonyms are used within the classroom.

As teachers, the danger is that we offer children words in a word bank or use an exciting scaffold that goes down well in an observation but really, they have only been supported superficially. Offering words up as alternatives is great practice, but I want to dive deeper into pupils' understanding.

'Give a man a fish and he won't go hungry today. Teach him to fish, and he will never go hungry again' is the old adage. The same is true with our teaching of synonyms and alternative vocabulary (let's be honest, any learning). Give our pupils a word bank and they will use it today – superficially. Teach them how, and why, and which word choices to make (supported by the word bank if required) and they will use those word choices incisively every day.

THREE MODELS OF VOCABULARY

Impoverished environments

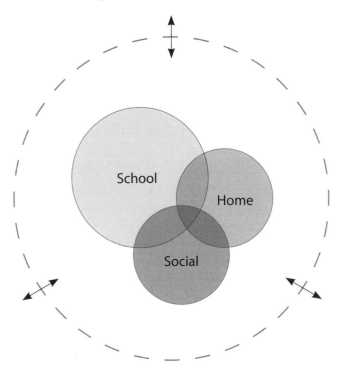

Rich environments

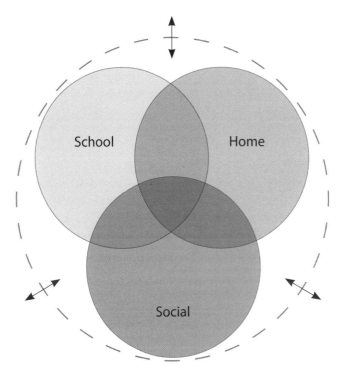

Impoverished rich environments

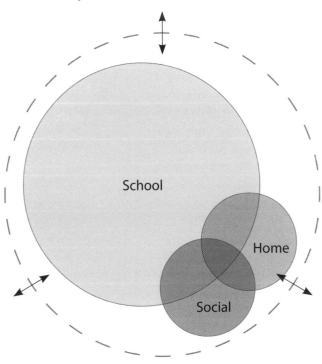

COLOSSAL FISH AND CHIPS

If synonyms are to be our infantry foot soldiers – the first line of attack and defence, against repetition and the mundane – then they need to be disciplined, highly-trained and deployed effectively by the Grand Master. For our youngest grasshoppers, it is certainly more appropriate for pupils to be made aware that there are lots of words in our language and that they can mean the same thing as each other or have very similar meanings. As pupils become older, we must introduce a variety of synonyms of increasing complexity. Depending on the context in which they are used, certain words may no longer be appropriate synonyms. For example, there are many ways to say 'big', and although 'big' and 'colossal' are synonyms, I wouldn't want pupils just replacing 'big' with 'colossal' at every opportunity. If this starts to happen, synonyms can quickly become a literary quicksand that learners become trapped by. We must dangle the vines from our vocabulary jungle and drag our pupils from its grasp, setting them free.

It is important that pupils understand that we are not just blindly replacing one word for another; sometimes the teaching or introduction of synonyms by teachers implies that this is true or possible. *'Synonyms are words that mean the same thing.'* Yes, this is true. But – and this is a significant but – this is wholly dependent on the context in which they are used. For example, if a pupil was eating a 'big sandwich', they might be eating a sandwich that is larger than their friend's sandwich or possibly larger in size than expected. Whereas, a 'colossal sandwich' might suggest that it is not only a much larger sandwich than expected, but also implies that it is of much greater quality and has more ingredients within the sandwich. (Maybe a ripe gherkin or two, with some continental meats and a carefully selected sauce-based condiment.)

Another food-related example: a 'big bag of fish and chips'. What about a 'colossal bag of fish and chips'? These do not mean the same thing. What does a big bag of fish and chips suggest? In my mind, a big bag of fish and chips means it wasn't the smallest available and that there is a good amount of chips and decent sized fish, nothing more. However, if you say 'a colossal bag of fish and chips', I see chips overflowing from the wrapper, an enormous fish with crispy batter, and salt and vinegar permeating the wrapped paper. There's no way you'll eat them all. It's a bag of chips to be savoured, a bag that will be talked about in weeks and months to come.

The point being made is that even though 'big' and 'colossal' are synonyms that denote how large a subject or object is, we must ensure that pupils begin to understand the subtle differences (the alternative meaning) that each synonym offers. Within the two food-based examples, we can quickly see how a pupil's skilled deployment of such words can help them add meaning and depth to a description, a conversation or a piece of writing. It will also add meaning when they read. The images that they will be able to build within their own mind will be subtler, more vivid and more enjoyable.

NOT SYNONYMS, RATHER... ALTERNATIVES

At this stage, it is important to understand that 'big' is a great word – there isn't anything wrong with 'big'. 'Big' only becomes a big problem when it is used as an adjective to describe *everything*. The pupils who are most likely to do this are the pupils who sit in the impoverished word pool model, and to a lesser degree the pupils who are found in the rich/poor word pool model.

In order to set them free, pupils need to understand the subtle differences of each word; we also want pupils to think carefully about what they are trying to say, i.e. what they are trying to accomplish by using that word. It should come as no surprise that this will require teaching and, more importantly, modelling. Learners must see examples, experiment, make mistakes, discuss their ideas and refine their understanding. We want older pupils to be able to use each word with meaning. To do this, they must understand the context they are trying to use the word in. By understanding that 'colossal' is a great *alternative* to 'big', rather than a synonym, pupils can start to make more meaningful and incisive word choices. Try offering words to pupils as *alternatives*, instead of synonyms.

N.B. It is important to note that Vocabulary Ninja is not asserting that you shouldn't teach synonyms. This aspect of the curriculum will still need to be taught and understood clearly by pupils.

It is important that teachers use the correct technical language with pupils. If you don't know (be honest), how can we expect the pupils to? #subjectknowledge

Especially within writing, I wouldn't hesitate to say that the increasing prominence of the SPaG curriculum and testing systems hasn't been particularly helpful. It is very mechanical. Synonyms are quite mechanical. If we just see them as one thing that simply replaces another, it implies that we have no freedom or control. It implies that there is no need for personal thoughts or creativity. And, because SPaG can be taught quite mechanically, the quicksand can once again take hold of our creativity and reduce it down to a box that can be ticked. We have to avoid this at all costs.

The next resource is an effective way of diving a little deeper into the subtle differences between words. The resource applies the synonyms within the same sentence – very similar to the fish and chips example – so that learners can see for themselves why a synonym might not work. Hate and detest would be considered strong synonyms with each other. However, hate and detest have subtle differences in their definitions and meanings; we cannot just swap one for the other blindly and assert that the same meaning is implied.

SCINTILLATING SYNONYMS

Words	hate (verb)	detest (verb)
Context	The children <u>hate</u> peas.	The children <u>detest</u> peas.
Definition	If you hate someone or something, you have a strong feeling of dislike for them.	If you detest someone or something, you dislike them with extreme negative emotion.
Difference	In the context of peas and children, hate is offering up a dislike, common to children, something they might say but could still be coaxed to eat them. However, if the children detest the peas, this is a much stronger feeling, perhaps they have caused illness previously, which the children remember. In this example, detest offers a more potent dislike of the peas. The children hate peas, <u>but still ate them</u>. The children detest peas, <u>so the peas had to be scraped from the plate</u>.	

SCINTILLATING SYNONYMS

Words	love (verb)	treasure (verb)	idolise (verb)
Context	I <u>love</u> this band.	I <u>treasure</u> this band.	I <u>idolise</u> this band.
Definition			
Difference			

SCINTILLATING SYNONYMS

Words		
Context		
Definition		
Difference		

SCINTILLATING SYNONYMS

Words			
Context			
Definition			
Difference			

SYNONYM MATCHING PAIR CARD GAME

like	lethargic	old	tropical	mature
assist	hot	lazy	similar	help

relocate	new	strong	delightful	mighty
sad	pretty	move	modern	glum

pink	green	charcoal	marmalade	mustard
yellow	orange	salmon	emerald	black

SYNONYM MATCHING PAIR CARD GAME

thrilled	excited	tearful	intrepid	fearful
unhappy	scared	brave	happy	ecstatic

cold	dark	brave	bitter	wretched
bad	angry	irritated	murky	daring

amazing	love	famous	elegant	frolic
beautiful	play	splendid	cherish	popular

ADVENTUROUS ALTERNATIVES

As discussed throughout the book, children often don't intentionally make poor or repetitive word choices. Quite simply, they have no other choice. As a teacher, you will have read thousands and thousands of pieces of pupils' writing and the same words will crop up over and over again. Once again, we must think about *why* this is happening, and quite simply, the children have no alternatives within their working word bank to draw upon. Words such as 'good', 'bad', 'happy' and 'sad' are far too common for Vocabulary Ninja's liking!

Vocabulary Ninja has endeavoured to provide alternatives for these nuisance words. In the Adventurous alternatives resource, you'll find 101 commonly overused words and 606 alternatives. The words in the far-left column are words that, as teachers, you will see and hear used all of the time. Pupils overuse these words because they have no other alternatives within their repertoire. This resource gives pupils a range of alternatives to use within their writing. When using such a resource, it's important to ensure that the words from the left column are not seen as words that we *can't* use. The only reason why we want to use alternatives for these words is that they are generally used in an overly repetitive manner. For example, not everything is 'bad' – bad isn't always the most appropriate word choice, though sometimes it will be. We want pupils to understand, use and remember alternatives for these sometimes-troublesome words.

Each alternative word is be ranked from Grasshopper to Grand Master (for fun – there is some level of increasing complexity, but not always). So, 606 pieces of prepared language for pupils to use, laid out in a way that can be simply photocopied and trimmed. These words may be contextually different, meaning they are not necessarily synonyms, depending on the context in which they are found and used.

All of the words found here are ideal to explore using the Vocabulary laboratory resources sheet on pages 51 and 52. Remember, a list alone is only so useful – we need to go all out ninja on each word to explore it, explain it, break it down, give it meaning in context. Eventually, your learners will become more ninja and do this for themselves.

ADVENTUROUS ALTERNATIVES

Grasshopper	Shinobi	Warrior	Samurai	Assassin	Grand Master
fantastic	incredible	remarkable	splendid	staggering	breath-taking
cross	fuming	annoyed	irritated	irate	exasperated
spectacular	glorious	astonishing	exceptional	sensational	phenomenal
awful	rotten	dreadful	wretched	vile	loathsome
appealing	elegant	enticing	angelic	ravishing	bewitching
large	vast	immense	oversized	mammoth	gargantuan
ink	soot	charcoal	onyx	jade	ebony
navy	sky	denim	peacock	teal	azure
dull	dreary	repetitive	tedious	monotonous	wearisome
heroic	daring	gutsy	intrepid	courageous	gallant
crack	smash	wreck	shatter	fracture	obliterate
wood	coffee	penny	chocolate	mocha	gingerbread
freezing	chilly	bitter	biting	arctic	sub-zero
arrive	near	join	reach	approach	advance
scream	weep	sob	bawl	yowl	whimper
unsafe	risky	perilous	hazardous	dicey	treacherous
dim	dusky	gloomy	murky	shaded	sunless
wreck	damage	impair	shatter	ravage	annihilate
taxing	demanding	challenging	exhausting	strenuous	back-breaking
simple	painless	elementary	effortless	uncomplicated	straightforward

ADVENTUROUS ALTERNATIVES

Grasshopper	Shinobi	Warrior	Samurai	Assassin	Grand Master
sweet	thrilling	impressive	remarkable	insane	unforgettable
eager	enthusiastic	roused	perky	ecstatic	aroused
dive	drop	tumble	descend	plummet	nosedive
well known	popular	leading	eminent	infamous	legendary
quick	speedy	rapid	nimble	blistering	breakneck
chubby	solid	overweight	plump	stout	rotund
spot	locate	notice	discover	acquire	pinpoint
flutter	hover	hang	float	glide	soar
fearful	alarmed	panicked	startled	spooked	petrified
pleasing	amusing	lively	entertaining	exciting	enthralling
collect	buy	gather	gain	obtain	acquire
vast	sizeable	tremendous	colossal	whopping	monumental
move	travel	visit	leave	continue	proceed
super	excellent	marvellous	exceptional	splendid	stupendous
lime	emerald	fern	moss	seaweed	pistachio
glad	delighted	thrilled	overjoyed	ecstatic	joyous
fear	dislike	loathe	detest	despise	execrate
keep	own	possess	boast	occupy	retain
support	aid	assist	guide	advise	contribute
stow	conceal	obstruct	shroud	camouflage	cache
hot	scorching	summery	blistering	roasting	tropical

ADVENTUROUS ALTERNATIVES

Grasshopper	Shinobi	Warrior	Samurai	Assassin	Grand Master
injure	damage	wound	incapacitate	maim	mutilate
gripping	compelling	fascinating	absorbing	captivating	spellbinding
jolly	cheerful	cheery	bubbly	effervescent	exuberant
leap	spring	hop	bound	bounce	gambol
slay	destroy	eliminate	decimate	massacre	exterminate
idle	work-shy	sluggish	slothful	inactive	lethargic
twin	alike	similar	related	equivalent	akin
small	teeny	tiny	minor	compact	delicate
glance	stare	gape	peer	inspect	examine
booming	thunderous	deafening	blasting	raucous	ear-piercing
prize	worship	cherish	idolise	treasure	adore
beautiful	attractive	appealing	magical	adorable	exquisite
cause	create	produce	concoct	assemble	fabricate
huge	enormous	vast	monstrous	towering	Herculean
carry	transport	transfer	shift	switch	relocate
crept	lurked	ambled	shuffled	dashed	manoeuvred
funny	strange	puzzling	curious	baffling	inexplicable
unused	fresh	pristine	current	modern	contemporary
enjoyable	lovely	thoughtful	likeable	admirable	congenial
elderly	ancient	mature	historic	tattered	frayed
carrot	tiger	fire	honey	marmalade	tangerine

ADVENTUROUS ALTERNATIVES

Grasshopper	Shinobi	Warrior	Samurai	Assassin	Grand Master
strawberry	rouge	rose	fuchsia	salmon	watermelon
interact	compete	frolic	cavort	engage	romp
charming	appealing	delightful	lovely	stunning	glamorous
plum	grape	jam	wine	violet	lavender
place	set	lay	deposit	position	plonk
swiftly	rapidly	speedily	briskly	hotfoot	lickety-split
calming	still	restful	soundless	serene	tranquil
actually	truly	genuinely	undoubtedly	certainly	unquestionably
cherry	scarlet	candy	blood	berry	crimson
rush	dash	scurry	scamper	hurtle	scuttle
unhappy	depressed	down	glum	blue	desolate
laughed	reported	stammered	thundered	insisted	acknowledged
afraid	fearful	nervous	panicky	alarmed	agitated
frightening	hair-raising	spine-chilling	daunting	formidable	blood-curdling
yell	cry	call	howl	bellow	shriek
nap	doze	rest	drowse	catnap	siesta
little	tiny	mini	minute	bijou	microscopic
suspend	cease	end	finish	conclude	terminate
mighty	meaty	powerful	robust	muscular	strapping
items	objects	property	gear	goods	possessions
foolish	ignorant	mindless	idiotic	moronic	brainless

ADVENTUROUS ALTERNATIVES

Grasshopper	Shinobi	Warrior	Samurai	Assassin	Grand Master
immediately	instantly	promptly	abruptly	swiftly	instantaneously
remove	steal	seize	grab	capture	pilfer
chat	gossip	blabber	speak	converse	natter
inform	notify	alert	warn	advise	declare
awful	dreadful	appalling	revolting	atrocious	sickening
next	afterwards	soon after	later	instantly	subsequently
muse	ponder	reflect	deliberate	meditate	ruminate
reasoned	pondered	considered	mused	deliberated	contemplated
plain	unsightly	deformed	hideous	menacing	grotesque
miserable	down	dispirited	despondent	tearful	forlorn
hugely	overly	mightily	exceedingly	immensely	desperately
stroll	saunter	amble	plod	wander	roam
feeble	frail	flimsy	powerless	fragile	delicate
uncanny	eerie	bizarre	unconventional	peculiar	surreal
moved	proceeded	progressed	journeyed	departed	travelled
snow	pearl	ivory	bone	powder	porcelain
gold	corn	banana	lemon	mustard	butterscotch
babyish	youthful	adolescent	childlike	immature	juvenile

PART 3

BE THE VOCABULARY NINJA

CONCLUSION

Words can be awe-inspiring, devastatingly painful, comfortingly unforgettable, intoxicating, humbling and so much more. Words are everything to me; words can be indescribably powerful for you. This is the esteem in which you now need to hold words – one where you hold them up to the highest level of importance in your classroom. Everyone has the potential to become a Vocabulary Ninja in body and mind. And, although this might feel like the end of our journey together, it's actually only the very beginning!

As this part of our journey together ends, you must start the next exciting instalment of becoming a Vocabulary Ninja by yourself. But you will never really be alone, I will always be here to support you, guide you and celebrate with you – just look to the Twitter-verse and you will always find me.

Recently, I was forced to look a little deeper into the definition of what a ninja actually is, and what the word itself means (yes, I hear the irony screaming loud and clear). Quite simply:

'A ninja is a person who excels in a particular skill or activity.'

No matter the context – whether it be dancing, singing, drawing, cooking, playing sport or bringing words to life as a Vocabulary Ninja – no-one can realistically expect to excel in a particular skill or activity without having the right mindset and the dedication to make their goals a reality. When you look at a skilled musician or sports person, you look on in awe as they execute their skills to perfection; they make it look easy. What you don't see is the meticulous preparation, the energy-sapping training or practise sessions, the heartbreaking disappointments and frustrations along the way. This will be true of your journey to become a Vocabulary Ninja teacher. Remember your training. Be micro-ambitious and strive for those marginal gains in every learning opportunity; the sum of all the small parts is where you will find your victory and have the greatest impact.

Who knows where the journey will take you. You are the trailblazing Grasshopper who is about to become a Vocabulary Ninja for yourself, your pupils and your school, and for that I applaud you. Believe it or not, your new focus will have an impact quickly, it will be noticed by the staff and pupils in your school. The *word* will spread! At this point, you will no longer be a Grasshopper, you will be Shinobi, and staff members will come to you for guidance to ask how you did it. It is then your responsibility to spread the Vocabulary Ninja mindset to *your* Grasshoppers. Truly, words will now have the power to unlock the doors to a whole new world of understanding in your school!

Good luck, although, I foresee that you will not need it.

Sayonara and namaste

(Goodbye and thank you. *'I bow to you.'*)

ADDITIONAL RESOURCES

Digital resources are essential in any modern classroom. That's why Vocabulary Ninja continues to provide a range of electronic apps to use on your tablets and smartphones. Go to page 6 for more information about more fabulous free resources designed to help pupils make independent vocabulary choices when they might be struggling.

WEBSITES

There are some brilliant resources around the web that can help you in your quest to improve pupils' vocabulary. Here are some of Vocabulary Ninja's favourites to get you started.

1 – Describing Words

www.describingwords.io

A wonderful resource for staff and pupils to access. The tool simply generates describing words (adjectives) for you to use.

2 – LiteracyShed / Spelling Shed

www.literacyshed.com

A vault of fantastic videos, perfect for inspiring writing. All with teaching ideas and techniques!

3 – Pobble365 and Pobble

www.pobble.com

Pobble is a terrific resource for supercharging pupils writing and creating a genuine audience for it. Pobble 365 offers a picture each and every day of the year with associated teaching ideas.

4 – Collins Co-Build Online Dictionary

www.collinsdictionary.com

A fabulously comprehensive dictionary resource with detailed yet child-friendly definitions of words, complete with examples, pronunciations and much more.

5 – NiftyWord

https://www.niftyword.com

Simply type in a word and NiftyWord will present you with associated suffixes, prefixes and related words! Super simple, but super effective.

6 – Etymology

www.etymology.com

Explore the etymology of any word you can imagine.

7 – Word Hippo

www.wordhippo.com

Explore synonyms, antonyms, meanings, rhyming and much more.

8 – Snappy Words

www.snappywords.com

An online visual dictionary and thesaurus.

9 – Lexipedia

www.lexipedia.com

A visual online synonym programme that displays associated words.

10 – Word Spy

www.wordspy.com

Want new words? Well, Word Spy brings them to you!

CONJUNCTION MALFUNCTION

Add the correct subordinating conjunction to the table below.

Clause 1	Subordinating conjunction	Clause 2
I felt ill during the journey	until	had a short nap and a drink of water.
Fred is tall and blonde,	whereas	his brother has long dark hair.
You won't succeed	unless	you work hard.
I love Elliot's work	because	he uses colour so precisely.
We played charades all evening	as	we had nothing else to do.
Claire has ridden horses	since	she was five years old.
She always feeds the cat	before	she goes to school.
I will be terribly sad	if	you leave me all alone in the house.
Lucy decided to go outside	even though	it was raining heavily.
Mary closed the shop	after	she drank some water.
The dog wanted to go for a walk	although	his owner wasn't so keen.
The class of children were happy	whenever	Mrs. Jones visited the school.
We couldn't go to the waterpark	because	it was closed today.
Don't go back into the building	until	it is safe to do so.
Danny tied his laces carefully	before	he ran onto the football pitch.
John had been listening carefully	whereas	Phillip hadn't paid any attention.

CONJUNCTION MALFUNCTION

Add the correct coordinating conjunction to the table below.

Clause 1	Coordinating conjunction	Clause 2
I am going shopping,	and	I am getting my hair cut.
Jerry wanted to make an apple pie	but	there were no apples left on the tree.
It was raining,	so	they went to the restaurant.
Oliver was a great striker,	but	he loved playing in goal.
Sam did not brush his hair,	nor	did he clean his teeth.
Claire hated peas,	yet	she still ate a spoonful.
Paul filled the bucket with water,	and	Mary dug a huge hole in the sand.
Fran studied a lot,	but	she didn't pass the test.
You can buy a new phone,	or	you can borrow my old one.
Daniel was hungry,	so	he ate a snack.
Jack was unkind to his friends,	but	he didn't mean to be.
I need to find a new job,	for	I am unemployed.
My dad doesn't like to cook,	so	he does it anyway.
He could go to school,	yet	he could stay at home.
I have got a bicycle,	but	I haven't got a scooter.
You can make your own costume,	or	just hire one from the shop.

ANSWERS

WHICH SENTENCE?

Which sentence uses **capital letters** correctly?	Tick one.
thomas, alex and mark visited London on Monday	
Thomas, Alex and Mark visited London on Monday.	✓
Thomas, Alex and Mark visited London on monday.	
Thomas, alex and Mark visited london on Monday.	

Which sentence is **punctuated** correctly?	Tick one.
Behind the door which was oak stood the phantom.	
Behind the door, which was oak, stood the phantom.	✓
Behind the door which was oak, stood the phantom.	
Behind the door, which was oak stood the phantom.	

Which sentence is **punctuated** correctly?	Tick one.
The little girl "squealed, I'm hungry and need feeding."	
The little girl squealed, "I'm hungry and need feeding."	✓
The little girl squealed, "I'm hungry" and need feeding.	
The little girl squealed, "Im hungry and need feeding."	

Which sentence uses **clean** as an **adjective**?	Tick one.
You should clean your teeth.	
Please clean your room before I arrive home.	
We need to clean the car today.	
His face was now extremely clean.	✓

Which sentence needs an **exclamation mark**?	Tick one.
The sky was bright blue	
She said the sun was so lovely	
What an amazing party that was	✓
The parks were extremely pretty	

WHICH SENTENCE?

Which sentence uses **coach** as a **verb**?	Tick one.
The coach rolled into the car park.	
The team were waiting for their coach to arrive to training.	
I will coach the junior team today.	✓
I would prefer to travel on the coach, rather than the train.	

Which sentence is the most **formal**?	Tick one.
You can come to my party if you wish.	
Please come to my party.	
Would you like to attend my party?	
I would be delighted if you could attend my birthday party.	✓

Which sentence contains an **embedded clause**?	Tick one.
The girl, who I met at the cinema, is in my class at school.	✓
The team is going to play on Saturday.	
Tom said he wanted to learn to ride a bike.	
Whenever they have time, they like to sit and read.	

Which sentence contains three **prepositions**?	Tick one.
Look around the corner and see who is coming.	
Tom is next to Fred, who is sat on the table near the door.	✓
Ellie has been waiting to visit the fair all week.	
Down by the river you can find all sorts of cool stones.	

Which sentence uses **park** as a **verb**?	Tick one.
Dad needed to park the car close to the entrance.	
Can we visit the park today?	
John scored his best time at the Park Run.	
They couldn't wait to get inside the waterpark.	✓

NOUN VS VERB

Decide if the target word is being used as a noun or a verb.

Target word	Context	Word class
crush	There was a crush in the corridor before playtime.	noun
bottle	We needed to bottle as much water as possible.	verb
paint	Everyone used the paint with care and attention.	noun
watch	His watch had stopped working.	noun
block	He raised his hand to block the sunlight.	verb
arm	They need to arm themselves before the battle begins.	verb
picture	He couldn't picture everybody playing nicely together.	verb
level	Jimmy used the spade to level off the ground.	verb
clap	Mr. Rogers could hear a clap, but wasn't sure where.	noun
peel	Next to the bin, there was lots of fruit peel on the floor.	noun
spoon	Helen was asked to spoon the sand into the tray.	verb
fire	There was a huge fire which could be seen for miles.	noun
light	As it was bedtime, Alex needed to switch off his light.	noun
dip	Peter wanted to dip his biscuit into the warm tea.	verb
cover	The book cover was tatty and frayed at the edges.	noun
book	Mum needed to book the tickets before they left.	verb
train	We need to train harder if we are to win the competition.	verb
frown	My frown just couldn't be turned upside down.	noun

SPaG FACTS

Give examples of these types of word.

noun	any person, place, thing
verb	any being, doing, having word
adjective	any describing word
adverb	can be added to a verb
pronoun	his, her, he, she, I, me, us, etc.
article	a, an, the
determiner	a, an, the, this, that, these
preposition	in, on, under, inside, next to
quantifier	some, any, many, few
concrete noun	bell, sky, blanket
abstract noun	truth, danger, happiness
collective noun	clan, herd, pack, troop
proper noun	capital letter name or place
coordinating conjunction	for, and, nor, but, or, so
subordinating conjunction	until, while, since, etc.
possessive pronoun	my, our, his, her, your

Rewrite these words in their expanded form.

can't	cannot
isn't	is not
won't	will not
couldn't	could not
mustn't	must not
didn't	did not
I'll	I will

Rewrite these words in the past tense.

kick	kicked
move	moved
catch	caught
remain	remained
fight	fought
perform	performed
blow	blew

Circle apostrophes for possession.

Jenny's car	We mustn't
I'll be late	Mark's dinner
The man's hat	Don't

Circle the modal verbs.

would	might
fill	park
should	may